LIVING FUTURES

Living Futures offers a fresh and exciting perspective on how people imagine and make futures as part of their everyday lives. It addresses important questions about who is included in futures thinking and futures making, and who is excluded.

Bringing together historical, anthropological, sociological, geographical and arts-based perspectives, this book provides a pithy yet expansive overview of social theories, research and creative approaches applied to futures thinking. Global practices and traditions of divination, fortune telling and speculation from antiquity to the present day are investigated for how they help people deal with uncertainty and engage with the yet-to-come, while also serving political and economic objectives. The book emphasises the plasticity of temporalities and lived experiences across diverse social groups, together with the role of the creatures, things, landscapes, and ecosystems with which we share our futures. The concluding chapter integrates the insights offered from each of the fields of research discussed in the book, providing ideas to spark vibrant and transformative approaches to creative futuring.

Living Futures will appeal to academics and students interested in the history, sociology, anthropology and geography of futures, futures studies, possibility studies, anticipation studies, design and forecasting, as well as anyone interested in how innovative social research and creative approaches offer new insights into futures thinking.

Deborah Lupton is SHARP Professor in the Faculty of Arts, Design & Architecture, University of New South Wales (UNSW) Sydney, Australia. Her research is interdisciplinary, spanning sociology, media and cultural studies and public health. She is located in the Centre for Social Research in Health and the Social Policy Research Centre, leading both the Vitalities Lab and the UNSW Node of the Australian Research Council Centre of Excellence for Automated Decision-Making and Society.

Shortcuts
Little Books on Big Issues
Series editor:
Anthony Elliott, Adelaide University, Australia

ABOUT THE BOOK SERIES:

Shortcuts is a major new series of concise, accessible introductions to some of the key global issues of our times. The series is developed as an A to Z coverage of emergent or novel social, cultural and political developments. Issues and topics covered range from food to fat, from climate change to suicide bombing, from hope to social futures. Whilst the principal focus of *Shortcuts* is the relevance of current issues to the social sciences and humanities, the books will also appeal to a wider audience seeking guidance on how to engage with today's leading social, political and philosophical debates. Short and concise, the books will provide cutting-edge insights into the pressing realities of our lives in these times.

Anthony Elliott is Distinguished Professor of Sociology at Adelaide University, where he is Executive Director of the Jean Monnet Centre of Excellence for Digital Transformations. He is Super-Global Visiting Professor at Keio University, Japan and Visiting Professor at University College Dublin, Ireland.

ALSO IN THE SERIES:

Freedom, 2nd Edition
Nick Stevenson

Hope
David Chandler

Living Futures
Deborah Lupton

Anti-Science
Dariusz Jemielniak

Food
John Coveney

Zombies
Jennifer Rutherford

Love
Tom Inglis

Panic
Keith Tester

Planet Sport
Kath Woodward

Global Finance
Robert Holton

Freedom
Nick Stevenson

Web 2.0
Sam Han

Suicide Bombings
Riaz Hassan

Feelings
Stephen Frosh

Confronting Climate Change
Constance Lever-Tracy

For more information about this series, please visit:
https://www.routledge.com/Shortcuts/book-series/SCUTS

LIVING FUTURES

SHORTCUTS TO A BIG IDEA

Deborah Lupton

Routledge
Taylor & Francis Group
LONDON AND NEW YORK

Designed cover image: iStock

First published 2027
by Routledge
4 Park Square, Milton Park, Abingdon, Oxon OX14 4RN

and by Routledge
605 Third Avenue, New York, NY 10158

Routledge is an imprint of the Taylor & Francis Group, an Informa business

British Library Cataloguing-in-Publication Data
A catalogue record for this book is available from the British Library

ISBN: 978-1-041-21307-9 (hbk)
ISBN: 978-1-041-21308-6 (pbk)
ISBN: 978-1-003-72657-9 (ebk)

DOI: 10.4324/9781003726579

Typeset in Sabon
by KnowledgeWorks Global Ltd.

CONTENTS

1

INTRODUCTION

Across human history and cultures, people have sought to engage with the future, often incorporating a potent mixture of religion, spirituality, magic, the occult, folk beliefs, philosophy and scientific knowledge. Whether described as the mantic arts, divination, soothsaying, fortune telling, speculation, prognostication, futurology, futurism, forecasting or prediction, these practices all involve peering into the realm of the yet-to-come and acting on the knowledge that is thereby generated. Today, the topic of futures remains a highly debated and researched area of study globally, as well as contributing to a wide array of professional activities such as foresight, predictive modelling, planning, financial investment and design. Future thinking is also part of contemporary everyday life. Members of the public engage in what I refer to as 'lay futuring practices', involving a multitude of techniques of thinking about, engaging with and making futures. They are planning for their own futures as they confront the serious and growing threats posed by climate change, loss of biodiversity, extreme weather events, outbreaks of novel or re-emerging infectious diseases, entrenched socioeconomic disadvantage, racism, armed conflict, displacement and the rise of populism and authoritarianism in the political sphere. Some individuals and social groups are actively engaging in counter-futures thinking as acts of resistance to prevailing imbalances of power, including creating new forms of community, activism and social movements for change.

DOI: 10.4324/9781003726579-1

There are many books by social researchers currently in print that include futures in the title. The word 'future' can be joined with any topic to denote a focus on the yet-to-come: for example, the future of work, education, families, the environment, health and medicine, gender and sexuality, technology. Any person, creature, thing or place can have a future, and one book cannot cover every future. I have chosen to give this little book the title *Living Futures*, signalling that its primary focus is on how people actively experience and imagine their futures as part of their everyday lives. The central tenet is that people's futuring practices are cultural, sociomaterial and biographical, embedded within their mundane routines as well as responding to extraordinary events. As this book is part of the Shortcuts series, it is short and to-the-point. I provide a pithy, yet expansive discussion of social theories and research applied to futures thinking that offer compelling insights into how people imagine and make futures. I explore how place, space and objects, together with cultural practices such as writing, art making, rituals and religious and scientific activities, have been developed and exchanged across the world as a way of transcending temporal boundaries and limits. Expert and lay futures thinking in past eras are also addressed, because how we have experienced the past inevitably shapes how we imagine and make futures.

This book therefore acknowledges the richness and creativity of 'non-expert' futuring that involves people applying their embodied and sensory knowledges of the world, together with their individual unique life histories, to imagine and act on their futures. This perspective acknowledges the grounding of futures thinking in the mundane nature of everyday life and simultaneously recognises the importance of the social structural, political and spatial contexts in which ideas about the future develop. By acknowledging the more ambivalent dimensions of affective responses to futures, such an approach goes beyond a perspective that positions feelings and imaginaries about futures as either utopian or dystopian. These affects include fear, despair, anxiety, grief, boredom, frustration, denial, detachment and, for some, sheer terror about the possibility of extinction of the human species or the world ending – but also hope and an eager expectation of something better. From this stance, future-oriented imaginaries and practices are both individual and collective, embodied and discursive, drawing on cultural repertoires passed on through generations as well as lived experiences.

In deciding what to include in this book, I attempted to focus on fresh ways of pondering and doing futures. The principle at the back of my mind throughout the writing process was that I would highlight theories, concepts and empirical studies that I considered to be most vibrant and paradigm-changing in the field of futures studies. I build on recent social and creative inquiry to argue for the reintroduction into futures thinking of approaches that recognise the importance of religious and mystical worldviews, creativity and speculative imagination. In adopting these perspectives, I aim to push the boundaries of futuring inquiry by making connections between historical eras, cultures and disciplines and seeing how these connections might generate interesting modes of conceptualising futures and futures thinking.

This book also emphasises the profoundly more-than-human dimensions of futures, recognising that our futures are shared with other humans, creatures and things. Futures are dynamic and fluid, comprised of entanglements between humans and the other living things (other animals, plants, fungi, microorganisms) with which we share our lives. In these ways, futures are lively, living and lived, full of affective forces that propel us to imagine, reflect on or seek guidance or clarity on what lies ahead in our own destinies. Living futures can also be interpreted as a hopeful way of thinking about the future, in which human life and that of the ecosystems of which they are part are sustained and flourishing. It is these concepts and modes of engaging in and experiencing futures thinking that I explore in the pages to follow.

SHIFTS IN FUTURING TECHNIQUES

These days, 'non-experts' frequently encounter utopian, dystopian and apocalyptic visions of what their futures may hold, issued from authorities such as government bodies, corporate consultancy agencies, think tanks and political leaders. For quite some time, and particularly since World War II, futures thinking in Western cultures have been dominated by positivist and quantified approaches that are viewed as the preserve of professional futurists (Andersson, 2018). Most disciplines directly focusing on futures thinking deploy neoliberal rationalist, strategic management, economics, decision making and systems theory, which are tied directly to capitalist, colonial and neoliberal economic systems (Demos, 2023; Son, 2015). These professional modes of future thinking concentrate predominantly on how organisations and corporate and government entities can predict and plan for futures on behalf of citizens, industry and other stakeholders (Barendregt et al., 2024).

The major forecasting techniques deployed by professional futures thinkers use equations and statistical methods such as modelling to find relationships between variables and make predictions about future outcomes. Other techniques – sometimes referred to as 'judgemental forecasts' – involve qualitative methods, including interviews with experts about their predictions, the Delphi method (iterative group discussions, usually with a panel of experts), scenarios (forecasts based on plausible scenarios) and horizon scanning (interviews or group discussions with experts together with document analysis to discern trends). However, these qualitative approaches are often described in professional futurism circles as being biased, less scientific or subjective compared with quantitative forecasting techniques (see, for example, Hyndman & Athanasopoulos, 2018).

Futures thinking has not always adopted these approaches. There have been various recent attempts to systemise and periodicise techniques of futuring to demonstrate how they have changed over time. Some of these reviews focus exclusively on Western traditions, while others incorporate techniques of futuring from other cultural contexts. Writing in the 1970s and in his role as part of the World Future Society, Edward Cornish (1977) acknowledged the rich traditions of divination and prophesising across global cultures ('the prehistory of futurism'), but considered the beginning of 'modern futures studies' to be characterised by the utopian tradition, which is directed towards identifying normative and preferred futures. According to Cornish (1977, p. vii), the times in which he was writing had led to the intensification of thoughts about the future, due to what he described as 'a maelstrom of social change' that had 'engulfed the world'. He outlined developments in the 'science of forecasting' as well as what he described as 'blunders' in this science, calling for the incorporation of methods such as social trend mapping and extrapolation, scenarios, models, games and simulations. Cornish (1977, p. vii) thought these approaches were essential to help government and corporate decision-making, prepare people to live in a changing world – and in more grandiose terms, were needed to build 'a greater civilization' and generate 'collective wisdom for mankind [sic]'.

Published four decades later, Wendy Schultz's (2015) 'brief history of futures' identified five waves of futures thinking across global cultures since prehistoric times: (i) the oral tradition; (ii) the early written age; (iii) enlightenment and extraction; (iv) systems and cybernetics, and (v) complexity and emergence. Of note is Schultz's description of the 'enlightenment and extraction' phase (taking place in the eighteenth and nineteenth centuries in Europe), as ushering in the idea of progress as a preferred future through science, technology and rationalism. She also observed that this period was characterised by technological and industrial development in pursuit of profit, with negative impacts on the environment. Schulz saw the twentieth century as the period when 'systems and cybernetics' approaches to futures took hold, with global events such as the Great Depression and World War II driving a desire to rebuild and plan for better futures. This was a time in which organisations such as the abovementioned World Future Society developed and rapidly expanded its membership. Schultz discerned the early stages of the fifth and latest wave – 'complexity and emergence' – as a period in which the technocratic and determinist approaches that had dominated since the 1950s were beginning to be challenged. New theories such as those from evolutionary psychology and integral philosophy (connecting science, religion and psychology) were exploring the 'inner spaces' of futures thinking, while the 'Pacific shift' had incorporated concepts and methods of futures from the Pacific Basin and Asia, leading to what Schulz characterised as more distributed and inclusive futures work.

In another review article published in 2015, but this time from a perspective outside the Global North, Korean scholar Hyeonju Son (2015) provided a useful overview of Western futures studies since the end of World War II, including its philosophical and historical contexts. Son identified three phases of Western future thinking, influenced by five intellectual traditions stretching back to antiquity: (i) religions; (ii) utopias; (iii) historicism; (iv) science fiction; and (v) systems thinking. According to Son's periodisation, the first phase of Western futures thinking (the period beginning in 1945 and stretching for two decades into the 1960s), was predominantly influenced by scientific inquiry and the rationalisation of futures. Techniques such as forecasting were developed, and futures studies moved from academic analysis to becoming framed as a way to develop a professionalised career as a futurist. Futures thinking during this time rejected traditional approaches such as utopian visions, grandiose evolutionary ideas, naive prophecies, science fiction, religious attitudes and mystical worldviews, seeing these as 'unscientific' and 'irrational'. During the second phase identified by Son (the 1970s and the 1980s), this scientific approach intensified and became more widespread, with globalised perspectives becoming dominant. Futures thinking across the world became even more influenced by corporate enterprise, rationalist economics and entrepreneurialism. Attempts were made by experts to generate normative visions of futures as part of the global project of wealth accumulation. According to Son, the neoliberal worldview that had emerged in the 1970s in Western governments went on to influence the third phase of futures thinking (the 1990s to the early 2010s). However, the approaches of foresight and critical futures studies demonstrated a more fragmented approach to futures thinking that took hold during this period. Corporatised futures practice was mostly applied to supporting strategic planning, while critical future studies practitioners sought to challenge these approaches, leading to what Son describes as 'an identity crisis' in futures thinking and an accompanying erosion of humanity-oriented futures inquiry.

A more recent overview of futures studies provided by Hungarian scholars (Kristóf & Nováky, 2023) offers some updates by including discussion of developments since 2015. The emergence of the COVID-19 pandemic in early 2020, they argue, provided the kind of global shock that inspired more futures thinking in relation to how the world might recover and what changes may occur in response. Kristóf and Nováky also reflect on how technological developments such as the rise of generative artificial intelligence (AI) tools may have an impact on quantitative futuring techniques. They have little to say about alternative techniques of futures thinking that involve creative qualitative methods. Nonetheless, there are encouraging signs that the scientistic and corporatised approach to future thinking, if not losing ground, has at least been challenged and augmented in the academic world of futures thinking by approaches from the humanities and social sciences that adopt a very different perspective. A notable policy change is evident in initiatives espousing that future thinking skills should not just be the preserve of experts but are relevant to everyone. This move is sometimes described as 'participatory futuring' or 'democratising' the future (Barendregt et al., 2024).

The notion of 'futures literacy' has been put forward as a key skill for people of all ages. Futures literacy has been defined most simply as 'the capacity to think about the future' (Liveley et al., 2021). A major futures literacy initiative is promoted by UNESCO, a United Nations specialised agency 'dedicated to strengthening our shared humanity through the promotion of education, science, culture, and communication' (UNESCO, 2025a). According to UNESCO, 'Being futures-literate empowers the imagination. It enhances our ability to prepare, recover and invent in the face of change'. UNESCO defines futures literacy as: 'help[ing] people understand why and how we use the future to prepare, plan, and interact with the complexity and novelty of our societies'. It goes on to explain that developing futures literacy can help people to 'escape the dominant narratives about the future and embrace new possibilities for action'. UNESCO identifies three types of futures – probable, preferable and reframed – and discusses the importance of people learning how to 'sense and make sense' of these types of futures, to be 'empowered' to be 'more creative, open, experimental and innovative' and to live with 'a higher degree of comfort with uncertainty and difference'. In pursuit of this goal, UNESCO has led the establishment of over 110 Futures Literacy Labs in 44 countries as well as supporting 37 UNESCO Chairs in Futures Literacy, Futures Studies and Anticipation in 31 countries (2025b).

In the interests of promoting futures literacy for the general population, futures thinking is now often presented in a simplified 'toolkit' form for the use of community organisations, schools and other groups. Some of these toolkits go beyond the standard methods and incorporate more creative approaches, but these are still rather limited rather than being truly adventurous. An example is the UK Government Office for Science's 'The Futures Toolkit' published in 2024 and made available as a public resource. The website hosting the toolkit defines futures thinking as 'a way of thinking about what's possible more deeply, honestly and strategically'. It describes it 'as much an art as a science' and, addressing potential citizen users, notes that '[y]ou will need to rely on creativity, intuition and insight, as well as research and analysis'. The website also contrasts futures thinking with forecasting and statistical modelling, which it notes tend to draw on historical data and trends to make predictions rather than imagining alternative futures that acknowledge the dynamics of change. Diversity of perspectives contributing to futures thinking (i.e., including not just experts in these conversations) is also championed.

The Toolkit itself includes the following techniques, all of which may be classified as judgemental forecasting. These are the Delphi technique; seven questions (an interview with seven questions to gather insights); horizon scanning; three horizons (helps explore the limitations of the present and identify different potential futures); driver mapping (charts and maps trends); SWOT analysis (identifies strengths, weaknesses, opportunities and threats of a policy, issue or event); scenarios; visioning (creating a common vision for the future); futures wheels (a structured brainstorming method); policy stress-testing (a method for testing policy or options against a set of scenarios); road-mapping (structured representations of the stages leading to a preferred future); and backcasting (determining the steps needed to deliver a preferred future). None of these approaches is particularly novel, creative or innovative, but they do go beyond the typical quantitative data-based approaches that are preferred by 'expert' forecasters.

Looking beyond these standard approaches, it is evident that futures thinking research and conceptual development in the humanities and social sciences is burgeoning and diversifying. An array of futures-oriented interdisciplinary fields of study and practice has emerged: possibility studies, utopian studies, extinction studies and anticipation studies among them. Scholars in the humanities have long been interested in futures as they are enacted across the creative and performing arts and in museum and curation practice. Design as a discipline has always been futures-facing with its focus on developing new goods or services, but the influence of speculative design has made a significant impact on creatively expanding this discipline's theories and techniques. Where once sociologists, anthropologists and geographers were reluctant to engage in theorising and empirically researching futures, there is now a strong literature developing in these disciplines. Across these fields and disciplines, scholars have begun to ask the question of who is included and excluded in futures thinking and futures making: whose futures matter? They are considering the sociomaterial and social structural dimensions of futures and identifying the regions and social groups that are viewed as expendable to future and those thought to be superfluous, as well as those who are simply ignored. These scholars are investigating how possible futures are often denied or disregarded because of the unsettling affects such imaginaries provoke, paralysing effective action at the individual and collective level to make better futures.

A number of key concepts and theories from these approaches provide meaning and depth to how living futures are understood and practiced in contemporary global societies. Each of these is detailed here:

more-than-human theory; chronodiversity; imaginaries, speculative fabulations, counter- and radical futurisms; and atmospheres, hauntology and weird futuring.

KEY CONCEPTS

More-than-human theory

There is evidence of a more-than-human turn in the humanities and social sciences in recent years which goes well beyond the traditionally human-centric focus of these fields of scholarship in the West. While the more-than-human theoretical perspective has often been referred to as 'new materialism', there is nothing new about it. It was a dominant worldview in Western societies before the Enlightenment and scientific revolution, remaining a central way of thinking in the Majority World and in First Nations' cosmologies.

More-than-human theory perspectives highlight the relational, dynamic, interwoven and non-linear dimensions of human/nonhuman worlds and temporalities. Sociomateriality is an integral concept in more-than-human theory, as it acknowledges the ways that humans come together with material things and spaces in assemblages, using their embodied senses and affective responses to generate capacities for action. The term 'entangled' is often employed to refer to the dense web of relations and assemblages of which all beings, including humans, are a part. Many nonhuman entities are considered to possess agencies and forces which are distributed between these agents and others (human or nonhuman) in the places and spaces in which they are located. Ways of being, knowing and learning are based in experiencing the complex more-than-human worlds through and with which humans move (Bawaka Country et al., 2023; Escobar, 2018; Hernández et al., 2020; Mabele et al., 2022; Redvers et al., 2024; Rots, 2017; Todd, 2016; Tynan, 2021; Yunkaporta, 2019).

Scholars engaging with more-than-human theory have identified how Western capitalist ideologies and practices seek to extract and exploit both humans and the other elements of the natural world (Pasternak et al., 2023). Relationality is at the heart of pre-Enlightenment, First Nations and contemporary Majority World perspectives, acknowledging the importance of respect and reciprocity with the ecosystems we share. The related concept of kinship is also important to more-than-human worldviews. Humans are positioned as part of kin relations with other people and other living things and objects, place and space. The concept of Land in Indigenous Canadian cultures (Redvers et al., 2024; Todd, 2016) and that of Country in Australian First Nations' worldviews (Bawaka Country et al., 2023; Tynan, 2021) encapsulates this viewpoint. Country/Land represents all the living creatures and geographical features in the landscape in which people reside or through which they move. Humans are considered as bound together with Country/Land, as guardians with obligations of care through relations of reciprocity. What harms humans, harms Country/Land, and vice versa (Bawaka Country et al., 2023; Redvers et al., 2024; Todd, 2016; Tynan, 2021).

Western scholarly inquiry, and particularly feminist materialism, has also sought to highlight these more-than-human relational connections, kinships and entanglements. Feminist technoculture theorist Donna Haraway's concept of 'natureculture' emphasises that nature and culture, rather than being binaries, are mutually constitutive. She contends that actors, whether human or nonhuman, are never pre-established; rather they emerge through relational encounters. (Haraway, 2003, 2016). Haraway has declared that she is not a posthumanist but a compost-ist (Haraway, 2015). By this statement, she means that she sees all agents in the world as richly interconnected ecosystems, including not only biological agents and geographical features but also human-made things. This approach blurs the boundaries between social structures and cultures, living creatures and the material world into which people are born, grow, move and eventually perish, becoming imbricated within the soil to contribute to other life.

Haraway's figuration of companion species can be employed to consider the relations and responsibilities of kinship we have with other species: ranging from other mammals to microorganisms. Haraway uses this term to describe the relationships that the human species has not only with other animal species but also with technologies. She has developed these ideas in key books such as the *Companion Species Manifesto: Dogs, People and Significant Others* (Haraway, 2003) and *Staying with the Trouble: Making Kin in the Chthulucene* (Haraway, 2016). The companion species trope recognises the inevitability of our relationship with other living things and the importance of learning to live together and to learn from each other. It suggests both the vitalities of these assemblages and also the possibility of developing a convivial relationship by recognising our mutual dependencies. Haraway points out that we are always located in time, space and place, and these spatial-temporal dimensions of our lives structure how we see the world and how we relate to the world in ways we cannot ignore. We see the world from a particular situated knowledge, a 'view from somewhere' and we must always 'stay with the trouble' (Haraway, 1988, 2016).

Jane Bennett is another key contributor to feminist materialism, devoting a particular focus to what she describes as the affects and vibrancies generated by human-nonhuman assemblages. She uses the term 'thing-power' to describe the vital power of human-nonhuman assemblages: 'the curious ability of inanimate things to animate, to act, to product effects dramatic and subtle' (2004, p. 351). Thing-power is a dynamic flow of energy between and with the components of assemblages. Bennett argues that the concept of thing-power emphasises the intimacy of humans and nonhumans, the ways that they are so closely intertwined in the moments when 'human being and thinghood overlap' (2004, p. 349). These assemblages create effects and affects that can be enabling or disabling. Identifying how thing-power is produced and its effects can go some way to better recognise 'the kinship between people and things' (Bennett, 2004, p. 360). Bennett is particularly interested in enchantment, and how this affective force drives humans' encounters with things and places. Her book *The Enchantment of Modern Life* (2001) is an attempt to understand how mundane activities and objects acquire and inspire strong affects that animate investments and attachments. Bennett (2001, p. 3) discusses these affects as contributing to the enchanting features of aspects of modern life, or what she describes as 'the wonder of minor experiences'. She contends that: 'To be enchanted is to be struck and shaken by the extraordinary that lives amid the familiar and the everyday' (Bennett, 2001, p. 4).

Engaging with these perspectives and concepts, we can begin to think about how futures are made with and through humans' encounters with the creatures, things and places with which they are entangled, and the powerful affective forces that are generated through these assemblages. We can see human futures as both collective and individually experienced, always shared, distributed and relational between human and more-than-human agents, constantly in the process of becoming, always situated in place and space.

Chronodiversity

The concept of chronodiversity is closely related to more-than-human theory. It refers to how time is a socially and materially constructed phenomenon, with diverse understandings of temporality evident across historical periods and cultural contexts. Contemporary Western societies rely on a concept of temporality that sees it as fixed, sequential and linear, extending from one time point to the next in a forward trajectory, as in the idea of the 'arrow of time' (Forbes, 2025; Thomas, 2025). This was not always the way that time was understood in the West. Before the invention of clock time (also referred to as 'hegemonic time') and the industrial revolution, temporality was conceptualised and experienced very differently (Adam, 2003, 2005). Indeed, philosopher of time Emily Thomas (Thomas, 2025) argues that while conceiving of time as a line may seem natural in Western thought, this conceptualisation is relatively new. The linear model of time existed prior to the nineteenth century, but it was thinkers in that century who were responsible for that model coming to dominate temporal worldviews.

Cyclical, pattern and fractal thinking in everyday life, cosmology and artmaking has been used across cultures and historical eras. They were embedded in knowledge systems via the elements of the natural world inhabited by people. Fractal thinking is a type of pattern thinking that emphasises the looping of time and space. It can be used to find order in complex systems and map how change occurs (Joye, 2011). The fractal is a recursive never-ending pattern, created through the repetition of a simple process and is responsive to non-linear processes: for example, the non-uniform shapes found in nature, such as trees, clouds, snowflakes, ferns, blood vessels or neuronal connections in the human body. Rather than events or experiences being sequential, for the cyclical model, time repeats itself, echoing natural processes such as the seasons, tides, moon phases and night and day. In ancient times and into the early modern period, time was viewed as circular, or wheel-like, with the past and the future viewed as inseparable: metaphorically 'a serpent devouring its own tail' (Ferkiss, 1975, p. 250).

The Stoic philosophers used this notion of time in their ethical approach to human action. They contended that there was no point attempting to change what we cannot control, given the events of the wheel of time repeat themselves endlessly (Forbes, 2025). In other Greek metaphysical thinking, the movements of celestial bodies were integral to understandings of time. For Plato, the wanderings of the heavenly bodies (nominated by him as the moon, the sun and five other stars) were connected to time. For Aristotle too, time was associated with motion. His concept of time depended on human embodied perceptions and mental responses to movement, together with the motions of the celestial bodies. Aristotle therefore saw time as circular, but with the past and future both open to human action (Forbes, 2025; Thomas, 2018, 2025).

The Aristotelian metaphysics of time was influential in twelfth-century Western philosophy, including in the thought of Galileo, Aquinus, Copernicus, Hobbes and Descartes. From the sixteenth century onwards, non-Aristotelian philosophies gradually developed, introducing absolutist accounts of time. The absolutist position presented time as an eternal, unchanging phenomenon that was independent of things, including motions, material bodies and human minds (with the possible exception of God). This perspective was evident in the writings of Thomas More in the mid-sixteenth century, and later, the scholarship of metaphysical scholars such as John Locke and Isaac Newton (Thomas, 2018, 2025). From the late eighteenth century onwards, the linear model began to prevail, spreading throughout the world as the hegemonic modality of understanding time. Thomas (2025) identifies four major developments contributing to this change: (i) chronography, or the visual representation of historical events as timelines; (ii) the theory of evolution, involving recognition of the existence and role of deep time; (iii) chronophotography, a new photographic art that could capture motion through successive images, thereby spatialising time; and (iv) advances in mathematics which added time as a fourth dimension of space.

Philosophies of time in other cultures challenge these notions of temporality. Contemporary First Nations cosmologies continue to view temporality as non-linear. This idea is referred to as 'everywhen' in Australian Indigenous cosmologies (McGrath et al., 2023). According to the concept of everywhen, 'time is neither exclusively linear nor cyclical but is "always" ... practices for knowing, remembering, and reenacting the past find embodiment in the present, blurring the distinctions of linear time and in some sense understanding the present as represented in a continuous now' (McGrath et al., 2023, p. 7). The symbol of the spiral encapsulates this conceptualisation of time. In Australian First Nations' knowledge systems, the use of song-spirals offers alternatives to Western concepts of time. Time is seen as multiple, agential and a manifestation of co-becoming (Bawaka Country et al., 2020, 2022). Similarly, in many Native American cultures, the concept of 'spiralling time' encompasses this idea, so that 'it makes sense to consider ourselves as living alongside future and past relatives simultaneously as we walk through life' (Whyte, 2018, pp. 228–229). Spiralling time is both cyclical and forward-moving, both predictable and irregular (De Vos, 2020; Whyte, 2018).

For Indigenous Australians, knowledge has been traditionally passed on through generations using pattern and relational systems thinking and placed-based and cultural memory practices, including storytelling, imagery (for example, paintings, stone carvings, woven objects or sand drawing), songs, rituals, dance and sacred sites embedded in Country. These practices, verified through collective sensing, feeling and instinct, form a living map that connects people and place and generates songlines. Tangible and narrative pathways store information and active knowledge into the future while maintaining a non-linear relationship with the past and present (Tempone-Wiltshire & Yunkaporta, 2025; Yunkaporta, 2019). This cosmology is constituted by continuing overlapping cycles within the physical context of Country. For example, in some Aboriginal kinship systems, a newborn child may be recognised as carrying the spirit of an ancestor, thereby linking past, present and future in connections between both ancestors and descendants. (Tempone-Wiltshire & Yunkaporta, 2025). By first establishing the patterning and temporal layering evident in these relationships and connections, and then looking beyond them, future thinking can eventuate. As Tyson Yunkaporta (2019, p. 91) argues:

> If you can see the relational forces connecting and moving the elements of a system, rather than focusing on the elements themselves, you are able to see a pattern outside of linear time. … If you bring that pattern back into linear time, this can be called a prediction.

In more recent eras, the Western perspective on time and the other agents in the world that are part of human life has been complicated by the development of post-Newtonian physics. Newtonian physics initially explained how the universe works relying on a mechanistic, deterministic and linear model of matter, time and energy. By contrast, quantum theory, introduced in the early twentieth century to investigate the properties and behaviour of molecular, atomic and subatomic phenomena, revealed the discontinuity and indeterminacy of matter, energy and time. It thereby unsettled assumptions about reality, knowledge, predictability, causality and temporality. In quantum theory, time is understood to be not singular, continuous or monolithic. Objects are viewed as relational and causality is indeterminate (Colman, 2023). In social theory, quantum theory has been applied beyond the molecular or subatomic level to macro systems, including those involving humans, by introducing these non-deterministic assumptions about people and their sociomaterial relationships with the world they inhabit, together with understandings of entangled and non-linear temporalities. It highlights the role that technologies/researchers play in any form of measurement, dissolving the notion of linear movement (including of time) (Colman, 2023; O'Brien, 2016).

Feminist philosopher and physicist Karen Barad is one of the most influential theorists who has brought together social theory with quantum theory. In their influential book *Meeting the Universe Halfway: Quantum Physics and the Entanglement of Matter and Meaning* (2007) and related writing (for example, Barad, 2003; Barad & Kleinman, 2018), Barad refers to the inseparability of the entanglements of space, time and matter(ing). As they (Barad, 2003, 2007) put it, matter and meaning are entangled, and it is through these entanglements that 'matter comes to matter'. Barad's concept of 'agential realism' recognises the relativity and indeterminacy of observations about the social and material worlds. Barad (2007) introduced the concept of 'intra-action' to describe the ways in which novel forms of agencies are relationally generated in human-nonhuman assemblages. Working together, they create affective forces and agential capacities for feeling, learning or action. Barad's idea of 'spacetimemattering' encapsulates the notion of the dynamic process of 'becoming' as humans intra-act with time. From this perspective, humans 'make time' by intra-acting with other agents.

Acknowledging chronodiversity leads to consideration of pattern thinking and relational systems thinking, involving devoting attention to how repetitive patterns and systems structure human thought and life and the rhythms of the living more-than-human worlds of which we are part. Taken together, this scholarship highlights that the future is open, due to all the uncertainties inherent in the ways that humans, other creatures and things intra-act with each other.

Imaginaries, speculative fabulations, counter- and radical futurisms

In futures research, the concept of social imaginaries positions them as collectively held constellations of speculations and narratives that draw on understandings, norms, values and experiences of the world. It is argued that social imaginaries are shared and situated, both individual and collective, embodied and discursive (Dawney, 2011; Stoetzler & Yuval-Davis, 2002). Generating imaginaries is a sociomaterial practice, as the act of imagining draws on people's embodied experiences and sensory engagements with the world. Indeed, the capacity to think and express imaginaries can be considered a human bodily affordance (Dawney, 2011). As Dawney (2011, p. 539, emphasis in the original) notes; 'Ideas and imaginings do not cause practice: they *are* practice'. Uncovering the contexts in which the imaginaries articulated by individuals are situated can be an insightful way of identifying the broader meanings, practices, norms and values that shape these imaginaries.

In another form of imaginary, Donna Haraway's (Haraway, 2011, 2013) concept of speculative fabulation invites us to engage in world-making – or what she terms 'worlding' – through futuristic storytelling that imagines possibilities beyond the present day. Inspired by feminist science fiction authors such as Ursula Le Guin and Octavia Butler, Haraway's approach brings together philosophy with creative writing. Haraway (2013) refers to her approach as 'multispecies storytelling of a feminist mode', bringing together 'the factual, fictional, and fabulated'. It is deeply intertwined with her commitment to social, multispecies and environmental justice. She develops an ethics of resistance to the current and future conditions of the more-than-human world, refusing to acquiesce to the apocalyptic permacrisis of environmental devastation that faces humans and nonhumans due to the profit-driven logics of late capitalism. Haraway emphasises the sociomaterialities of these speculative worlds, noting that 'It matters what relations relate relations. It matters what worlds world worlds. It matters what stories tell stories' (Haraway, 2016, p. 35).

Most of Haraway's writing introduces this kind of speculative fabulation, as she plays with ideas and words in her practice of worlding and subversive futures thinking. An example is one of her best-known pieces, an essay entitled 'Manifesto for cyborgs: science, technology, and socialist feminism in the 1980s' (Haraway, 1985), in which she outlined the speculative figure of the cyborg (inspired by science fiction) as a metaphor to encapsulate her theories of natureculture and more-than-human embodiment. Haraway's cyborg manifesto outlined a political position in which the normative dualisms of self and other, male and female, mind and body, idealism and materialism, humans and other creatures, or humans with things such as technologies, are dissolved. Haraway draws attention to the idea that human ontologies must be understood as multiple and dynamic rather than fixed and essential, as blurring boundaries between nature and culture, human and nonhuman, self and other. The cyborg metaphor encapsulates this idea, not solely in relation to human-technology assemblages, but to any interaction of humans with nonhumans. In *Staying with the Trouble: Making Kin in the Chthulucene* (Haraway, 2016), Haraway suggests the Chthulucene as a convivial speculative fabulation that helps humans better understand the ways forward for mutual flourishing with the other entities in ecological assemblages. She developed the term from the Greek word for earth and the species name for a spider that inhabits the Californian ecosystem in which Haraway lives. For Haraway, it is a better word than Anthropocene, as it encapsulates the tentacular and myriad temporalities, spatialities and mutual dependencies in planetary kinship relations.

The practice of counter-futuring, initially described by Jussi Parikka (2018), involves alternative ways of envisaging futures that recognise chronodiversity, cultural diversity, avoid colonialist and othering in futures thinking and attempts to avoid the binary between utopian and dystopian imaginings by retaining fluid, open-ended possibilities. Another term used in some critical futurism approaches is that of 'radical futurisms'.

Radical futurisms adopts an activist praxis from political economy and decolonising theory. Exponents of this approach advocate for an 'emancipated chronopolitics' that actively challenges the normative concepts of futures that are underpinned by the capitalist economic system, the oppression of marginalised peoples and exploitation of other creatures and the environment for profit. This position calls for inserting considerations of decolonisation, social and multispecies justice-to-come into futures thinking (Demos, 2023).

For Yin Paradies (2020), who identifies as Anglo-Asian-Aboriginal and is a descendent of the Wakaya peoples of the Gulf Country, Australia, decolonisation involves awareness of colonial pasts and presents as well as working towards a future that is free from the colonial past. He characterises decoloniality as generating 'truthful futures' (Paradies, 2020, p. 441), requiring the removal of colonisation before a range of possible futures can be opened up for First Nations peoples. Paradies also suggests the rupture of the meaning of the terms 'settlers' and 'Indigenous peoples' in a proposed future in which all people return to the land and make amends for the ravages of coloniality: what Australian Indigenous peoples refer to as 'caring for Country'. Paradies predicts a cataclysmic event due to humans' destruction of the environment in which global civilisation will be extinguished, potentially making way for small-scale self-organised communities based on anarchist political structures and meaningful connections with the natural world. This activity will involve a disinvestment from extractivist modernity and capitalist systems to achieve 'viable and vivacious ex-modern futures in which we decolonise to both survive and thrive' (Paradies, 2020, p. 447).

Queer futurism is another radical approach, building on theories of queer temporalities that have developed since the early years of the twenty-first century. Some of the queer futurism scholarship has argued for a kind of 'untimeliness', adopting the notion of 'queering' as a way of challenging and problematising dominant rhetorics and practices: in this case, of futurity. From this perspective, queerness is portrayed as a collective modality of futures thinking (McBean, 2013). Other queer theorists see futures thinking as a way of developing a radical optimist approach. From this position, futures thinking offers possibilities for escaping the heteronormative and often downright homophobic present, in which queer people, and especially those who are living with disability, are people of colour or in socioeconomically disadvantaged circumstances are subjected to everyday violence, stigma and marginalisation.

For José Esteban Muñoz, for example, queerness was seen as always already futuristic, a state of not-yet-becoming, as outlined in his book *Cruising Utopia* (Muñoz, 2009), where he issued an urgent call for reviving the queer political imagination. Munoz (2009, p. 1) began his book with the phrase '[q]ueerness is not yet here. Queerness is an ideality. Put another way, we are not yet queer'. He went on to describe the future as 'queerness's domain'. Muñoz explained that the project of queerness should be to see, feel, enact and imagine new ways of being beyond what he sees as 'the quagmire of the present', rejecting the here and now, which he viewed as confining and perpetuating inequalities without any radical vision for what should change. The importance of developing concrete rather than abstract utopias was another key argument. Concrete utopias are related to historically, politically and materially situated struggles, such as those between the hegemonic social class and the underclass, that lead to collective action to achieve better futures for the oppressed.

For futures thinking, these theoretical perspectives help us to further consider chronodiversity and chronopolitics and stimulate creativity in configuring counter- and radical futures that can disrupt current ways of being. We can think about how social/sociotechnical imaginaries and visions of futures are generated and distributed, the power relations and vested interests that are embedded in these imaginings, whose futures are privileged in dominant modes of futures thinking, and who are excluded.

Atmospheres, hauntology and weird futuring

Another direction of thought in social and cultural theory lies in understanding the non-representational or ineffable atmospheric dimensions of human experience and understanding. The concept of affective atmospheres has a strong focus on the sociomaterialities of human experiences as they come together with place, space and other people and things inhabiting or moving through these spaces. In more-than-human theory, affect refers to the intensities that are part of these relations. Building on Spinozian and Deleuzean scholarship, affects are considered to be distributed forces that are generated and shared with and through people's encounters with human and nonhuman agents. Affects are therefore mobile, distributed and dynamic, constantly subject to change as people move through time and space (Thrift, 2004; Vannini, 2014). Affective atmospheres are intensities of feeling that are distributed and sociospatial, mutually generated between people and nonhuman actors, contributing to 'making matter come to matter'. The practices of sensing through human embodiment and the emergence of intensities of feelings from these practices are integral to the production and experience of affective atmospheres (Anderson, 2009; Bille & Simonsen, 2021; Thrift, 2004).

There is nothing more affective, multisensory and ineffable than the entities that haunt us. Western social and cultural theory concerning hauntology and spectrality became popular following the publication in 1994 of the English translation of Jacques Derrida's book *Specters of Marx* (Derrida, 1994/2012). As the book's title suggests, Derrida examined how in relation to Marxist thought the past continues to haunt the present. He used the term 'hauntology' to refer to the form of scholarship that investigates the dimensions of this persistence of the past in the present and into the future, with particular reference to unfulfilled or abandoned future visions. Hauntology refers to blurred temporal boundaries. For Derrida, understanding what is not easily discernible or is ineffable (such as ghostly traces of ideas) was important for consideration of the present and the future. His figure of the revenant alludes to a concept drawn from ancient supernatural thinking about the return and repetition of the past into the present and the future, demanding a reckoning from the living for past wrongs.

In response to Derrida's book, there has been an outpouring of scholarship, particularly in literary studies, cultural studies and other fields of the humanities that investigated how haunting the spectral and the ghostly could be considered as conceptual metaphors for human consciousness. Cultural theorist Mark Fisher (2012) built on Derrida's writing to develop the concepts of the *no longer* (an event or entity haunting the present from the past) and the *not yet* (haunting the present from the future). Both concepts challenge the notion of the unbroken progression of linear time, thereby foregrounding temporary disjuncture. For Fisher (2012, p. 16), '[t]he future is always experienced as a haunting'.

In an essay, Barad (2010) has drawn hauntological theory together with quantum theory in the attempt to disrupt dominant concepts of continuity. They use their term 'intra-action' to describe these discontinuities and disjointedness of temporalities, writing the essay in a way that interweaves different historical periods so that the position of the reader of the essay is not assumed to be in the here-and-now. For Barad, the quantum behaviour of electrons is itself a queer spectral form of temporality, as it challenges Newtonian assumptions about causality, time, place and space, and the division between nature and culture. She points out that Derrida's concept of hauntology and spectrality similarly posits that the past is never closed. To address the past and future is to speak with ghosts in a way that is responsive and responsible for the entangled relations of inheritance and to open to relations of indeterminacy for what is to come in terms of social justice. Spacetimematter can be productively reconfigured.

Weird futuring is a term used by Bahar Noorizadeh (2022) in a similar way to Parikka's counter-futuring. She challenges the contemporary positivist, corporate and rationalist approach to future thinking that is demonstrated in most methods, and notes that opportunities to think about and intervene in futures is mostly limited to those who employ these methods. They are based on assumptions and information about what is knowable and calculable. Weird futuring, by contrast, looks to creative practices such as those demonstrated in the genre of weird fiction, which plays with the uncanny, the dark, the strange and the supernatural or un-natural to produce unexpected future imaginaries. Indeed, many lay futuring practices rely on these disturbances and affects to create ideas about the future.

Future thinking approaches that incorporate the weird, the unseen, the not-quite-there, the occult, the uncanny and the supernatural can generate forceful visions of the future. Such atmospheres are vibrant, suffused with powerful affects and embodied responses that prickle our skin, raise our hackles, shock or disturb us. These approaches offer suggestive ways for uncanny queer and counter-futuring to be explored, including the idea of plural utopias that are oriented towards the unfamiliar and the unknown and to open, fluid futures. They make us feel otherwise in ways that may help us recognise and acknowledge the affective forces and spectres of the past as we imagine our futures.

THIS BOOK

Each chapter in this book stands alone as an introduction to a disciplinary approach to futures but complements the others to build a narrative about living futures and creative futuring. These days, the boundaries between disciplines are very porous, and many scholars identify themselves as multidisciplinary or interdisciplinary (myself among them). But for the sake of organisational clarity, I have chosen to structure the book in this way. Chapter 2 presents an overview of histories of futures, providing examples from past eras and across cultures. Then follows Chapter 3 on anthropologies of futures and Chapter 4 on sociological and geographical inquiry. Chapter 5 is interdisciplinary, presenting a range of creative futuring methods from the arts, speculative design and pedagogies, as well as the domains of curation and museology. The brief concluding chapter draws together the main themes and concerns of the book and suggests ways forward for exciting new ways of imagining and making futures in social research. Taken together, the chapters integrate social and cultural theory and creative practice as they are applied to futures thinking. The importance of more-than-human modes of understanding and cosmologies that challenge the dominant contemporary Western concept of time are emphasised throughout. The book shows how each discipline can draw on each other, providing examples of the kinds of innovative theory and research methods that can be used to understand how people and social groups across time periods and cultures understand, imagine and prepare for futures: that is, how they live futures.

REFERENCES

Adam, B. (2003). Reflexive modernization temporalized. *Theory, Culture & Society*, 20(2), 59–78.

Adam, B. (2005). *Timescapes of modernity: The environment and invisible hazards*. Routledge.

Anderson, B. (2009). Affective atmospheres. *Emotion, Space and Society*, 2(2), 77–81.

Andersson, J. (2018). *The future of the world: Futurology, futurists, and the struggle for the Post Cold War imagination*. Oxford University Press.

Barad, K. (2003). Posthumanist performativity: Toward an understanding of how matter comes to matter. *Signs*, *28*(3), 801–831.

Barad, K. (2007). *Meeting the universe halfway: Quantum physics and the entanglement of matter and meaning*. Duke University Press.

Barad, K., & Kleinman, A. (2018). Intra-actions. *Mousse*, *34*, 76–81.

Barendregt, L., Bendor, R., & van Eekelen, B. F. (2024). Public participation in futuring: A systematic literature review. *Futures*, *158*. https://www.sciencedirect.com/science/article/pii/S0016328724000302

Bawaka Country, Burarrwanga, L., Ganambarr, R., Ganambarr-Stubbs, M., Ganambarr, B., Maymuru, D., Lloyd, K., Daley, L., Suchet-Pearson, S., Wright, S., Tofa, M., & Hammersley, L. (2023). Bala ga' lili: Communicating, relating and co-creating balance through relationships of reciprocity. *Social & Cultural Geography*, 24(7), 1203–1223.

Bawaka Country, Burarrwanga, L., Ganambarr, R., Ganambarr-Stubbs, M., Ganambarr, B., Maymuru, D., Lloyd, K., Wright, S., Suchet-Pearson, S., & Daley, L. (2022). Songspirals bring country into existence: Singing more-than-human and relational creativity. *Qualitative Inquiry*, *28*(5), 435–447.

Bawaka Country, Wright, S., Suchet-Pearson, S., Lloyd, K., Burarrwanga, L., Ganambarr, R., Ganambarr-Stubbs, M., Ganambarr, B., & Maymuru, D. (2020). Gathering of the clouds: Attending to indigenous understandings of time and climate through songspirals. *Geoforum*, *108*, 295–304.

Bennett, J. (2001). *The enchantment of modern life: Attachments, crossings, and ethics*. Princeton University Press.

Bennett, J. (2004). The force of things: Steps toward an ecology of matter. *Political Theory*, 32(3), 347–372.

Bille, M., & Simonsen, K. (2021). Atmospheric practices: On affecting and being affected. *Space and Culture*, 24(2), 295–309.

Colman, F. (2023). Quantum feminicity: Modes of countermanding time. *Technophany. A Journal for Philosophy and Technology*, 2(1), 1–37.

Cornish, E. (1977). *The study of the future: An introduction to the art and science of understanding and shaping Tomorrow's world*. Transaction Publishers.

Dawney, L. (2011). Social imaginaries and therapeutic self-work: The ethics of the embodied imagination. *The Sociological Review*, 59(3), 535–552.

Demos, T. (2023). *Radical futurisms: Ecologies of collapse, chronopolitics, and justice-to-come*. Sternberg Press.

Derrida, J. (2012). *Specters of marx: The state of the debt, the work of mourning and the new international*. Routledge. (Original work published 1994).

De Vos, L. M. (2020). Spiralic time and cultural continuity for indigenous sovereignty: Idle no more and the marrow thieves. *Transmotion*, 6(2), 1–42.

Escobar, A. (2018). *Designs for the pluriverse: Radical interdependence, autonomy, and the making of worlds*. Duke University Press.

Ferkiss, V. (1975). Christianity and the fear of the future. *Zygon*, *10*(3), 250–262.

Fisher, M. (2012). What is hauntology? *Film Quarterly*, *66*(1), 16–24.

Forbes, G. A. (2025). Is the future open? In N. Emery (Ed.), *The Routledge companion to philosophy of time* (pp. 251–260). Routledge.

Haraway, D. (1985). Manifesto for cyborgs: Science, technology, and socialist feminism in the 1980s. *Socialist Review*, *80*, 65–108.

Haraway, D. (1988). Situated knowledges: The science question in feminism and the privilege of partial perspective. *Feminist Studies*, *14*(3), 575–599.

Haraway, D. (2003). *The companion species manifesto: Dogs, people, and significant otherness*. Prickly Paradigm.

Haraway, D. (2011). Speculative fabulations for technoculture's generations: Taking care of unexpected country. *Australian Humanities Review*, *50*(5), 1–18.

Haraway, D. (2013). SF: Science fiction, speculative fabulation, string figures, so far. *Ada: A Journal of Gender, New Media, and Technology*, 3(1), https://hdl.handle.net/1794/26308.

Haraway, D. (2015). Anthropocene, capitalocene, plantationocene, chthulucene: Making kin. *Environmental Humanities*, 6(1), 159–165.

Haraway, D. (2016). *Staying with the trouble: Making kin in the chthulucene*. Duke University Press.

Hernández, K. J., Rubis, J. M., Theriault, N., Todd, Z., Mitchell, A., Country, B., Burarrwanga, L., Ganambarr, R., Ganambarr-Stubbs, M., Ganambarr, B., Maymuru, D., Suchet-Pearson, S., Lloyd, K., & Wright, S. (2020). The creatures collective: Manifestings. *Environment and Planning E: Nature and Space*, 4(3), 838–863.

Hyndman, R. J., & Athanasopoulos, G. (2018). *Forecasting: Principles and practice*. OTexts.

Joye, Y. (2011). A review of the presence and use of fractal geometry in architectural design. *Environment and Planning B: Planning and Design*, 38(5), 814–828.

Kristóf, T., & Nováky, E. (2023). The story of futures studies: An interdisciplinary field rooted in social sciences. *Social Sciences*, 12(3). https://www.mdpi.com/2076-0760/12/3/192

Liveley, G., Slocombe, W., & Spiers, E. (2021). Futures literacy through narrative. *Futures*, 125. https://www.sciencedirect.com/science/article/pii/S0016328720301531

Mabele, M. B., Krauss, J. E., & Kiwango, W. (2022). Going back to the roots: *Ubuntu* and just conservation in southern Africa. *Conservation & Society*, 20(2), 92–102.

McBean, S. (2013). Queer temporalities. *Feminist Theory*, 14(1), 123–128.

McGrath, A., Troy, J., & Rademaker, L. (Eds.). (2023). *Everywhen: Australia and the language of deep history*. University of Nebraska Press.

Muñoz, J. E. (2009). *Cruising utopia: The then and there of queer futurity*. New York University Press.

Noorizadeh, B. (2022). Weird-futuring. *Counter-N*, 12. https://doi.org/10.18452/24452

O'Brien, K. L. (2016). Climate change and social transformations: Is it time for a quantum leap? *Wiley Interdisciplinary Reviews: Climate Change*, 7(5), 618–626.

Paradies, Y. (2020). Unsettling truths: Modernity, (de-)coloniality and indigenous futures. *Postcolonial Studies*, 23(4), 438–456.

Parikka, J. (2018). Middle East and other futurisms: Imaginary temporalities in contemporary art and visual culture. *Culture, Theory and Critique*, *59*(1), 40–58.
Pasternak, S., Cowen, D., Clifford, R., Joseph, T., Scott, D. N., Spice, A., & Stark, H. K. (2023). Infrastructure, jurisdiction, extractivism: Keywords for decolonizing geographies. *Political Geography*, *101*. https://www.sciencedirect.com/science/article/pii/S0962629822001779
Redvers, N., Lokugamage, A. U., Barreto, J. P. L., Bajracharya, M. B., & Harris, M. (2024). Epistemicide, health systems, and planetary health: Re-centering indigenous knowledge systems. *PLOS Global Public Health*, 4(8), e0003634. https://doi.org/10.1371/journal.pgph.0003634
Rots, A. P. (2017). *Shinto, nature and ideology in contemporary Japan: Making sacred forests*. Bloomsbury Publishing.
Schultz, W. L. (2015). A brief history of futures. *World Future Review*, 7(4), 324–331.
Son, H. (2015). The history of Western futures studies: An exploration of the intellectual traditions and three-phase periodization. *Futures*, *66*, 120–137.
Stoetzler, M., & Yuval-Davis, N. (2002). Standpoint theory, situated knowledge and the situated imagination. *Feminist Theory*, *3*(3), 315–333.
Tempone-Wiltshire, J., & Yunkaporta, T. (2025). Contributions from aboriginal Australian psychology: Songlines, memory, and relational knowledge systems. *Psychotherapy and Counselling Journal of Australia*, *13*(2). https://doi.org/10.59158/001c.143975
Thomas, E. (2018). *Absolute time: Rifts in early modern british metaphysics*. Oxford University Press.
Thomas, E. (2025). Spatializing time: How the long nineteenth century turned time into a line. In N. Emery (Ed.), *The Routledge companion to philosophy of time* (pp. 87–98). Routledge.
Thrift, N. (2004). Intensities of feeling: Towards a spatial politics of affect. *Geografiska Annaler*, *86*(1), 57–78.
Todd, Z. (2016). An Indigenous feminist's take on the ontological turn: 'ontology' is just another word for colonialism. *Journal of Historical Sociology*, *29*(1), 4–22.
Tynan, L. (2021). What is relationality? Indigenous knowledges, practices and responsibilities with kin. *Cultural Geographies*, *28*(4), 597–610.

UNESCO. (2025a). *UNESCO in brief.* https://www.unesco.org/en/brief

UNESCO. (2025b). *Futures literacy & foresight.* https://www.unesco.org/en/futures-literacy

Vannini, P. (2014). Non-representational ethnography: New ways of animating lifeworlds. *Cultural Geographies*, 22(2), 317–327.

Whyte, K. P. (2018). Indigenous science (fiction) for the Anthropocene: Ancestral dystopias and fantasies of climate change crises. *Environment and Planning E: Nature and Space*, *1*(1–2), 224–242.

Yunkaporta, T. (2019). *Sand talk: How indigenous thinking can save the world.* Text Publishing.

2

HISTORIES AND FUTURES

HISTORIES OF TEMPORALITIES

Chapter 1 provided an overview of the philosophy of time and how concepts of temporalities have changed since antiquity. As noted in that chapter, for ancient Greek philosophers, temporality was seen as cyclical, following the rhythms of nature. It was not only philosophers who relied on their observations of the natural world to conceptualise time. Prior to the rise of humanism and the Enlightenment in Europe, Western cultures adopted a perspective on the world that was profoundly animist, seeing their bodies and selves as interwound with the weather, the seasons, the earth, waterways, atmospheres, celestial bodies and other living creatures. The humoural model, involving the importance of maintaining balance between the four humours in the body and the external 'non-natural' factors such as air, water and diet, portrayed people's health and wellbeing as integrated with the natural world. People's embodied perceptions and sensory engagements with climactic conditions and the ecosystems of which they were part were central to their lived experiences of time as they moved through their life course (Hartnell, 2018; Lupton, 2012; Thomas, 1984).

In medieval Europe, time was measured by the cyclical rhythms of the seasons, moon phases and weather patterns, and the human activities that were aligned with the natural world. Circadian rhythms governing wakefulness and sleep, together with observations of the cycles

DOI: 10.4324/9781003726579-2

of the seasons and change, decay and death in humans and other living things, all contributed to people's rich understandings of timescapes. People's daily life rhythms were variable and dynamic, responsive to and entangled as they were with cultural practices and routines as well as the variations in weather, climate conditions and the other elements of ecosystems (Adam, 2003; Adam, 2005). However, Christianity brought in a very different viewpoint on nature, temporality and human destiny by offering the possibility of individual salvation, allowing a person to escape from history to eternity in Heaven and leading to collective redemption of humanity within history. Pre-Christian beliefs persisted into the early modern period and beyond, but Protestant Christianity increasingly sought to portray humans ('Man') as superior to and separate from the natural world. Other living things became objectified as resources to be subjugated by humans to meet their own needs, and humans were positioned as unique species reigning over all others (Thomas, 1984). The other Abrahamic faiths, Judaism and Islam, espoused similar principles about human salvation. The Enlightenment took up these principles and transformed them into the secular idea of human progress through scientific development (Ferkiss, 1975; Thomas, 2025).

The invention of the clock, and with it, clock time, was a integral transformation in the ways that global societies and cultures have understood, experienced and practised time (Adam, 2003, 2005). The first mechanical clocks were developed in the fourteenth century, located in towers in villages and towns so that local residents could hear the tolls that marked time periods throughout the day. Clock-time logic was promoted in medieval monasteries as a way of keeping monks disciplined and free from 'natural' impulses so that they could better serve God (Adam, 2003, 2005). It was integrated with emerging metaphors of human bodies as mechanical entitities that ideally are less subject to the vagaries of nature, with moral judgement assigned to those who were viewed as lacking appropriate tight control of their bodies (Lupton, 2012). Built on abstract, fixed mathematical principles decontextualised from the temporalities and rhythms of the fleshly human body and the natural world, the clock measured time according to precise hourly segments. It imposed a rhythm on people's everyday life that had previously been shaped by their own bodies and that of the natural environment and celestial phenomena in which they lived (Adam, 2003, 2005).

Since then, clock time (also referred to as 'hegemonic time') has become normalised and commodified, central to the post-Enlightenment processes of rationalisation, mass industrialisation, modernisation and globalisation that have transformed everyday lives across the world. Time became money as the capitalist ethos intersected with clock time. It has been used to delimit chronodiversity, colonalise non-Western societies and impose on them Western temporal values and practices. Clock time is represented as the most appropriate and efficient way to structure human lives so that they are productive according to the ethos of capitalism. Those who fail to live up to the norms and expectations of clock time are penalised, represented as lazy, unpunctual, undisciplined and unproductive (Adam, 2005).

The implications of clock time can be seen in the development of concepts of chance, probability, risk and other forms of quantifiable futures thinking techniques that replicated its rationalist, abstractified and linear concept of temporality. Philosopher Ian Hacking, in his book *The Taming of Chance* (1990), wrote about these changes as they pertained to the science of statistics emerging at the end of the seventeenth century together with merchantile capitalism. He argued that Enlightenment thought saw superstition and beliefs about chance as irrational, whereas scientific statistical laws could be established to manage and predict outcomes: or as his book title puts it, to 'tame chance'. In such approaches, there is a clear discourse about controlling the future by predicting it with forms of quantification. In terms of how the future is imagined, clock time as used in capitalist speculation sees the future as the extended present, a resource that can be managed by human action for profit (Adam, 2003). As Adam (2003, p. 73) puts it: 'This means a radical present-orientation makes parasitic use of the future – our own and that of successor generations'.

ANCIENT DIVINATION

For millennia, and across global cultures, ideas about the future and human destiny were predicated on notions of fate and fortune, often linked to the will or punishment of the gods. In antiquity, expert diviners and oracles forecast the future in response to both individual and collective futures. They observed and interpreted patterns in the natural world and paid attention to occurrences that seemed to be out of the ordinary, thought to be initiated by supernatural forces – the gods – as warnings or evidence of good fortune. It was believed that individuals themselves could also manifest supernatural signs in their bodies that could be interpreted in various ways by the professional diviner. Mediums of supernatural forces could also be other living things, manifesting signs that required expert interpretation (Beerden, 2014; Driediger-Murphy & Eidinow, 2019).

Necromancy, or 'divination by the dead', was one common practice. The belief underpinning necromancy was that the spirits or souls of the dead were closer to the divine than living humans and therefore had privileged access to the supernatural. It was closely related to practices of ancestor worship. People attempted to communicate with the dead in the afterworld to gain direction on what the future held. There were various practices employed to summon the spirits of the deceased. In ancient Greece and Rome, necromantic practices included communicating with apparitions of the dead either awake or in dreams, using mediums who were possessed or inspired by the departed, using objects to contact them or engaging with the corpses or body parts of the dead to force their spirits back to speak to the living (Heiduk, 2022).

Other divination methods included forms of animal entrail divination ('haruspicy') and prodigy-interpretation (considering the meaning of extraordinary natural events such as earthquakes, strange lights, comets, disease outbreaks or the births of deformed animals or humans) (Beerden, 2014; Driediger-Murphy & Eidinow, 2019). The practice of extispicy, most prevalent in Mesopotamia, was a form of haruspicy, involving an expert ('haruspex') examining the entrails of a sacrificial sheep. The haruspex would first address the oracle gods with prayers and benedictions, requesting them to write their message on the sheep's entrails. The haruspex would then examine the organs of the animal to determine whether there were any deviations from the normal state, shape, and colouring, or patterns. If abnormal features or patterns were observed, the haruspex would interpret their meaning as favourable or unfavourable omens in terms of what the gods were communicating about their will (Daneshmand, 2022).

Observations of the behaviour of birds (augury) featured particularly strongly in the ancient world. As creatures that inhabited the skies, birds' behaviour was understood to be controlled by gods or atmospheric spirits: the birds therefore embodied these supernatural forces. So important were birds to ancient Greek and Roman divination practices that several of the words we now use in English for fate, divination or fortune telling stem from the Greek or Latin for birds. The word omen comes from the ancient Greek word for eagle, the special bird of the god Zeus, and other large, high-flying birds of prey. Several English words for good luck, prosperity, guidance and divination stem from the Roman Latin *auspicium* ('bird watching for omens'): for example, augur, auspicious and auspices (Zuesse, 1975).

In ancient Greece and Rome, there were special places where people could go to consult diviners or oracles. For example, at Delphi, a female oracle, Pythia, acted as the medium for the words of the god Apollo, her words interpreted by the priests at the site. The clients of the oracle would leave questions to be answered, including whether a family member would be cured of an illness, a harvest would be bountiful, or a new occupation or place of residence would work out well (Beerden, 2014). In the sanctuary of Heracles, pilgrims gave prayers to the god, cast dice and then used an interpretation text provided there to ascertain the meaning of the dice (Braekman, 1980). Scrying, or peering into a reflective surface to look for shapes or patterns as omens, was also a common practice. At the sanctuary of Demeter at Patras, a mirror was lowered into a spring and various rituals were performed together with interpretation of images on the mirror to reveal whether a person of interest was alive or dead (Voss, 2014).

In Roman culture, it was believed that all deities ruled the destinies of humans. The goddess Fortuna, who ruled luck and chance, was thought to influence how people's lives would unfold (her name remembered in the English words for luck or chance, 'fortune', 'fortunate' and 'fortuitous'). Jupiter was considered as the all-powerful father, with the greatest of all divine powers. He was believed to send auguries spontaneously to any Roman citizen, but experts (magistrates and augurs) could also solicit signs from him through rituals. Once these signs were identified, they were used to prove Jupiter's will and his assent to activities such as the creation of priests or decisions about going into battle. These divination methods were used primarily as tools of the elite: to enhance magisterial, senatorial or imperial authority, calm potential civil unrest and assist Roman people in dealing with uncertainty, feelings of lack of agency or comprehending social and political change (Driediger-Murphy, 2019;

Stiles, 2019). As one example, the phenomenon of 'tree portents' played a role in helping Roman society manage crisis and uncertainty. Tree portents included withering trees being revived and then flourishing upon an emperor's arrival into a city, or a tree springing up outside an emperor's house. In these cases, the trees were believed to signify imperial success and good fortune for an army or a city (Stiles, 2019).

The notion that humans' behaviour could pre-empt or mediate divine decisions about their fortune was evident in the ancient Mediterranean world. Making offerings to the gods, reciting or writing incantations or using charms, figurines and amulets were all ways of attempting to intervene in the future by preventing misfortune or enhancing the probability of good fortune. These objects were made of materials such as papyrus, linen cloth, metal and clay. For example, in Mesopotamia, clay or wood monster figurines were made to keep in houses and used together with rituals and offerings to deflect evil forces and attract the presence of benign beings that would bring with them good fortune. In ancient Rome, amulets made from bronze or precious metals, animal bones or teeth, amber and gemstones were worn as protective charms (Boschung & Bremme, 2015). While the Old Testament and the Hebrew scriptures officially condemned magic and divination, there were many references to such practices therein, demonstrating influences from other cultures nearby. These include portrayals of seers and prophets/prophetesses in favourable ways as transmitters of God's oracles using methods such as dream interpretation, necromancy and divination by casting lots or reading signs in a sheep's fleece. People used these oracles to predict features of everyday life: whether they would get married, have children, make a safe journey, recover from an illness or locate lost property (Jeffers, 2007).

The practice of astrology is believed to have originated in Babylon (modern Iraq) in the early fifth century BCE, employed to create horoscopes based on people's birth date. As a systematic study of celestial bodies, astrology developed in Egypt in the second century BCE, then passed into Greek and Latin societies and into the Byzantium, Islamic and Latin West cultures. Astrology as a science was developed by Claudius Ptolemaeus (Ptolemy) in second-century Alexandria, who compiled an influential treatise on the topic. He divided the 'science of the stars' into two parts. The first considered the theory of the heavens and the second was devoted to its practical application to the world below (that inhabited by people) (Carey, 2010).

In India, astrological and other divinatory beliefs can be traced back to the Vedic civilisation. Similar to ancient Mediterranean beliefs, prognostications and omens were regarded as a means of knowing the future by observing phenomena occurring on land, in the atmosphere and celestial bodies. These signs were viewed as messages from the gods, hinting at impending disasters caused by humans' sinful deeds. Once identified as portents by sages, these troubles could then be averted by human action, such as engaging in appropriate religious rituals involving prayers, praise and offerings to the gods. Sages were often kept under royal patronage to interpret these signs. Divination texts provided guidelines for interpretation were available, with the earliest known example the *Gargasaṃhitā*, estimated to have been written in the first century BCE. This text lists various omens portending disaster, many of which have close parallels to Mesopotamian cuneiform texts which had been translated into an Indian language in the fifth and early fourth century BCE (Beinorius, 2017).

In ancient and early China, the cosmology behind futuring practices was based in ancestor worship, the concept of Mandate of Heaven, Taoism and Legalism. During the Shang dynasty (1766–1045 BCE), divination beliefs and practices were dominated by ancestor worship beliefs. The spirits of dead people were believed to live on in the afterworld, with power to influence the fortunes of the living. The use of oracle bones was a type of necromancy, involving recording queries about the future on ox bones or turtle shells, burning these in a fire, and interpreting the pattern of cracking from heat exposure as signs from the ancestors. The *I Ching* (the Book of Changes), composed by Shang dynasty's King Wen, was available to be used by all citizens as a way of foretelling their futures. It contained a system to predict the future using fundamental truths, including the interplay of *yin* and *yang*: opposing forces in the universe which together form order in the universe (*Tao*). The concept of Mandate of Heaven (*Tianming*) presented an alternative approach to relying on the supernatural powers of the ancestors. It was influenced by the moral philosophy of Confucius, Mencius and Lao Tzu, which posited that the future would only be assured if all people followed certain precepts, adhering to the highest ethical standards. In its turn, Taoism challenged the Mandate of Heaven by arguing for the importance of returning to the simplicity of following the natural cycles of life to achieve harmony. It conceptualised the future as a perpetually changing dialectical paradox, where the patterns of nature could be observed in concert with the five elements of change (wind, earth, fire, metal and water). Legalism then emerged towards the end of the Warring States Period (475–221 BCE), with the rise of the Qin dynasty. Under the principles of Legalism, ordinary people were not able to decide or control their own future – it was governed on their behalf by the Emperor (Hoffman, 2013).

The ancient Chinese practice of *feng shui* (translated as 'wind-water') has been practised in China for thousands of years, spreading into other East Asian cultures over that time. *Feng shui* is a form of geomancy, or divination using signs from the natural landscape. It brings together

Confucian, Taoist and Buddhist thinking, rooted in the theory of *qi*, *yin* and *yang*, and the five elements. The central tenet of *feng shui* is that the earth is a lively, breathing entity, an organism like the human body that requires free flows of energy (*qi*) to flourish. The interaction between *yin* and *yang* creates change. The goal of *feng shui* masters is to balance *yin* and *yang* by organising and complementing landscapes in ways that to allow positive energy to flow freely throughout a space, thereby creating a harmonious physical environment that will lead to good health and fortune. These principles were employed when making decisions about where best to site building works, with many imperial buildings and ancient Chinese cities located, oriented and designed according to *feng shui* guidance (Zhang, 2018).

THE MEDIEVAL AND EARLY MODERN PERIOD

The early medieval period was characterised in many European regions by a mixture of pre-Christian with Christian beliefs in the supernatural and the occult. Numerous methods of divination and prognostication entered the Western world in the Middle Ages from ancient Near East cultures, including in early Judeo-Christian texts. By the seventh century CE, books of divination had been developed in places such as Egypt which combined pre-Christian with Christian ideas about fate, including the notion of prayer to God and the saints as a way of achieving a desired outcome (Braekman, 1980). In medieval Europe, it was believed that relics of the Christian saints' bodies (such as their bones), rituals, amulets, incantations or prayers addressed directly to the saints empowered these supernatural beings to intercede in people's destinies by averting ill-fortune or demonic powers. Ancient Roman beliefs about the Goddess Fortuna underpinned the symbol of Fortune's Wheel, which re-emerged in the

Middle Ages in Europe to represent the powerful and unpredictable nature of fortune. Fortuna was believed to spin this wheel randomly, meaning that certain people would prosper and others would suffer depending on where it stopped. Later uses of Fortuna appeared in Christian times in illuminated manuscripts and other artworks such as sculptures and stained-glass windows in cathedrals, and in early tarot cards (Brendecke & Vogt, 2017).

One temporal concept from ancient Celtic thought is that of thin places/events: places and happenings where the divide between the mundane and the divine/other world/the unseen is gossamer thin. Such places included ancient burial mounds, caves, voyaging across the sea, islands or the places behind waterfalls, requiring humans to find a portal to traverse from one place and time to another (Béres, 2012; Healy-Musson, 2019). A study of supernatural beliefs and practices in early medieval Ireland found that despite the strong presence of Christianity, concepts about the Otherworld and the entities believed to live there from pre-Christian times continued to flourish, including the use of material artefacts such as amulets and talismans to avert evil or bring good luck. Objects such as animal bones, and prehistoric flint arrowheads and stone axes were used for such purposes (O'Sullivan, 2017). Necromancy was also practised across Europe in medieval times, remaining a common way to elicit predictions about the future and often incorporated into Christian belief systems. Cemeteries, as liminal spaces and thin places harbouring both the living and the dead, were key places where necromancy rituals were carried out. They were also connected with the interpretation of auspices concerning such matters as predictions of the deaths of community members (Heiduk, 2022).

Viking Age and early medieval Northern European concepts of the future were strongly influenced by Old Norse mythology. According to this cosmology, the concept of fate or destiny was structured through the actions of the gods and female supernatural beings: the *nornir* or *norns*. The *norns* were portrayed as representing the past, present and future, determining humans' destiny. Fate was used discursively to provide explanations for problematic events or social or political relationships and removing responsibility for these misfortunes from the people to whom they occurred. In medieval Scandinavian culture, fate also operated as a narrative instrument and as part of religious belief and divination rituals (Meylan, 2014). Old Norse sources describe destiny as discerned by individuals through omens or prophetic dreams: often as interpreted by dying figures, embodying a liminal condition in which they were able to access the realm of the unknown or the invisible. People's fate could also be influenced by the curses of others or those embedded in objects such as stolen treasure and things enhanced by the powers of the gods, or incurred by transgressive behaviour such as flouting cultural norms or kinship obligations. The concept of destiny therefore was an expression of social tensions and obligation, operating to establish moral boundaries to which people were expected to adhere (Páez, 2024).

Astrology was revived in medieval Europe as part of the return to Greek philosophy and scholarship in the northern and Italian renaissance of the fifteenth century. Most of the precepts of astrology used in Europe came from the Arabic-speaking world. After the fall of the Roman Empire, while astrological knowledge declined in the Latin West under the rule of the Romans, Arabic astrology flourished through scholarly interchanges between the Islamic world and Byzantium, which combined Greek natural philosophy with pre-Islamic Arabic, Indian, Jewish and Persian sources. Astrology became the bedrock of intellectual inquiry in the Islamic world during this time, influencing developments in astronomy, mathematics, music, medicine, alchemy, magic, philosophy, theology, literature, calligraphy and the arts.

Professional astrologers were included in rulers' courts and frequently consulted as experts (Carey, 2010).

Astrology permeated most dimensions of medieval thought, including science and medicine. Zodiac Man/ *Homo signorum* ('man of signs') is the most ubiquitous of medieval medical depictions of the human body in Western Europe, the Middle East and Asia, showing the relationship of celestial phenomena to the human body (Strådal, 2016; Wee, 2015). Images of this Zodiac Man appearing in medical texts and almanacs depicted 'melothesia': the idea that the stars, the moon and the planets had a direct influence on the human body. They typically showed a male human body with the signs or names of zodiac entities superimposed on or adjacent to the body parts they were thought to influence. These images were used as tools by healers to determine when would be the best time to provide medical treatments such as bloodletting or herbal remedies (Strådal, 2016).

In his influential book *Religion and the Decline of Magic*, historian Keith Thomas (1973) outlines popular beliefs about religion, magic, superstition and science in early modern Britain (the sixteenth and seventeenth centuries). As Thomas demonstrates, in Britain, the boundaries between religion, magic and superstition have historically been extremely porous. For example, before the Reformation, Catholic beliefs and practices incorporated pre-Christian magical beliefs, practices and rituals. By the early modern period, however, theological scholarship and practice frowned upon such notions, representing them as heathen because they flouted the concept that God himself ruled humans' fortunes: not the working of nature, nor luck nor chance. It was insisted that people's destinies was not a lottery but rather the consequence of God's orderly purpose for individuals: His divine providence and will (Thomas, 1973). This opinion was clearly expressed in the words of Oliver Cromwell, who declared that the word fate should not be used, as 'it was too paganish a word', while theologians argued that even natural processes themselves (such as disease outbreaks or harvest failures) were nothing but the 'very finger of God working through his creatures' (Thomas, 1973, p. 92).

Nevertheless, as noted in Thomas' book (1973), various time-honoured modes of prediction and fortune telling remained well-used in Britain in this period. These included systems for weather and harvest forecasting and prognostication based on the assessment of probabilities related to recorded information or formulae incorporating the day of the week on which certain key religious or natural events fell (the twelve days of Christmas, saints' days and moon phases). Divination based on traditions such as physiognomy (face reading) and palmistry (palm reading), which interpreted bodily signs of individuals' destiny, were popular. Other methods used calculations based on readings of the Spheres of Light and Death, which consisted of circles divided into compartments. Private divination systems used by fortune tellers (often referred to as 'cunning' women or men) relied on such signs and patterns as the croaking of frogs, the behaviour of corn on a hot hearth or reading coffee grounds, while lay people were aware of the significance of omens such as unusual dreams, cloud formations or chance encounters with animals. Astrology was viewed as a systematic way of explaining human behaviour or predicting events. Ordinary people also frequently paid astrologers to help them make major life decisions or make predictions about their futures, such as if they would marry, become pregnant, die in childbirth or receive an inheritance.

Edward Bever's book *The Realities of Witchcraft and Popular Magic in Early Modern Europe* (2008) includes a chapter on divination and prophecy: characterised by Bever as 'beneficent magic'. As his analysis makes clear, people in northern Europe were intrigued by witchcraft and magical practices, both fearing them and using them for the purposes of future thinking. Bever describes how people mostly used these methods as part of mundane life, with the occasional spectacular manifestation of magical activity. Common practices were the interpretation of omens, dreams or prophesies, or scrying, which involved using reflective surfaces such as mirrors, glass objects, buckets of water or crystal balls, and staring into the reflection until an image appeared that could be treated as a divinatory sign. Another method, called sieve driving, was used to identify thieves or witches. It involved balancing a sieve on the tip of a pair of shears that were held upwards while the names of suspects were recited. When the sieve began to rotate, this was taken to denote the guilty party. This technique was common across northern Europe and Britain. Some people employed diviners to help manage their business affairs. Others used divination to locate lost relatives or a thief, foresee the success of a potential marriage, or determine whether misfortune was due to witchcraft.

The advent of forms of mass printing together with improvements in literacy contributed to the dissemination of futuring practices among the population. In early modern Europe, many printed materials were available to those who were literate (and featuring woodcut illustrations for those who were not) that rendered and reproduced dire predictions of future events. For example, German-language broadsheets, pamphlets, books, personal diaries and correspondence and tracts during the sixteenth century Holy Roman Empire described extraterrestrial events that were deemed to portent destruction to come on earth. Prognostications repeatedly drew connections between celestial movements and anomalous events such as comets, solar halos, shooting stars and eclipses (referred to as *Wunderzeichen*, or 'wonder-signs') that signified God's message that the end of the world was nigh (Dukes, 2025).

In Britain, almanacs as printed forecasting media were extremely popular among most social groups – from the nobility and educated people to farmers. Almanacs were mass-produced ephemeral books, often centred around the coming calendar year. They included details of regular events such as astronomical events, tides, exchange rates and feast days and festivals, but also information to help with astrological forecasting about politics, the weather, the state of crops, population health and personal horoscopes. Other popular handbooks using various methods of prognostication helped readers make predictions about the future and to choose days that might be most favourable to carry out important activities. In these books, the changing phases of the moon were considered to be particularly influential on people's destiny: including the phase that was current at the time of their birth or when their marriage ceremony was conducted (Thomas, 1973).

The strong connections between emerging science, philosophy, religion, magic and divination were notable during the Tudor period. For example, in the sixteenth-century courts of Henry VIII and Elizabeth 1, astrologers were frequently consulted to determine the most propitious dates for major events. John Dee, an astrologer and alchemist, was a favourite of Elizabeth I, used by her for consultations about propitious decision-making. Dee was one of several thinkers in Europe during this time who were developing early scientific methods in their efforts to study natural laws together with the occult and esoteric practices to make sense of how the universe operated beyond the accepted Christian cosmologies (Clucas, 2006). The combination of neo platonic, Pythagorean and Kabbalistic philosophy in Dee and others' scholarship at this time has been referred to as the 'Hermetic Tradition'. This approach combined esoteric beliefs about the Greek god Hermes and the Egyptian god Thoth, traced back to 300 BCE. According to the Hermetic Tradition, humans were represented as microcosms of earthly and heavenly worlds with the capacity and free will to shape their own destinies and even reach divine levels in the 'Great Chain of Being'. These beliefs were revived in fifteenth century Europe as part of the new humanism of the Renaissance, contributing to the proto scientific movement into the sixteenth century that sought a syncretic approach bringing together all knowledge: theology, natural philosophy and ethics (Szönyi, 2014). Dee was well connected with other Renaissance scholars in countries such as France, Poland and Italy who were working towards developing similar natural philosophy theories: some of whom also enjoyed the patronage of royalty for their learned advice. Indeed, some historians view Dee as a leading contributor to the emergent scientific revolution in England and Europe (Clucas, 2006).

In the East, astrology and other forms of divination remained important in the medieval and early modern period, underpinned by local religious and cosmological beliefs. In medieval and imperial China, divinatory practices were used across the population. Professional diviners played a crucial role in maintaining the social order, providing people with ways to deal with fears and uncertainties, and acting as a middle path between their clients, the communities in which they lived and the cosmologies offered by Buddhist, Confucian and Taoist perspectives (Zongli, 2022). Fortune telling based on Eastern astrology has been popular in Japan since the Edo period (1600–1868 CE). Eastern astrology is based on a nine-star system and the client's date of birth, with a special calendar used to make predictions about that individual's destiny (Kentarō, 1995). The Mongolian *Manual of Astrology and Divination*, copied sometime in the 1800s but likely to be portraying knowledge that was already many centuries old, depicts a Buddhist approach. The manuscript is replete with charts and diagrams imported from Tibet to Mongolia in the late 1700s. This information was designed as aids for Mongolian Buddhist monks to calculate auspicious times to carry out important actions, such as departing on a journey. The manual features drawings of mythical creatures, celestial bodies and numerical calculations related to their movements and influence, as well as diagrams of the human body to demonstrate the influence and location of these forces and how they affected people's health (North, 2015).

THE POST-INDUSTRIAL AGE

The eighteenth and nineteenth centuries are often characterised in history and popular culture as the 'age of science': a time in which rational, humanist thinking had superseded superstition and magical beliefs. Yet numerous historians and social anthropologists (Bell, 2007; Pooley, 2024; Sneddon, 2019; Waters, 2015) have contested this claim, pointing out that these beliefs and related practices persisted in Britain, Ireland and continental Europe well past the Enlightenment and the industrial revolution, including among the middle- and upper-classes. They note the re-emergence in Victorian times of a fascination in spiritualism, the occult, mesmerism, astrology and fortune telling, involving a re-packaging of the magical using pseudo-science, as well as lingering beliefs in magic and witchcraft in Europe, Ireland and Britain into the twentieth century. These phenomena suggest continuity and transformation rather than a decline in magical and superstitious thinking.

In his book *The Magical Imagination*, Karl Bell (2012) shows how magical beliefs and practices – or what he refers to as 'the magical imagination' – were prevalent in England from the late eighteenth century until the outbreak of World War I. Bell argues that the magical imagination was vital as a cultural resource to help English working-class people adjust to or resist the rapid changes of the industrial revolution. The supernatural elements of the magical imagination offered possibilities for people to think otherwise, both individually and collectively, by distancing themselves from mundane reality. For Bell, therefore, the magical imagination was a form of agency in conditions where many felt powerless: a way of providing a sense of control and an impetus towards social action in challenging and uncertain times where the usual ways of living and social institutions were falling away. The magical imagination also challenged the divides between magic, religion and science, as well as the distinction between 'traditional' and 'modern', or 'superstition' and 'rationality'. During this period, spiritualism, clairvoyance, astrology and other occult and divination practices became popular again, while new customs, including tarot card interpretation, were invented.

After losing popularity and scientific credibility by 1700, astrology was revived as a mode of divination in the nineteenth century. A popular English almanac, entitled *The Prophetic Messenger* and published under the pen name 'Raphael', included a chart of daily planetary positions. In 1825, the same author published the book *The Astrologer of the Nineteenth Century: Or the Master Key of Futurity, being a Complete System of Astrology, Geomancy & Occult Science*: the lengthy subtitle clearly demonstrating the book's focus on divination. Other futuring practices described in the book included necromancy, celestial omens that foretold historical disasters, magic rites, charms and incantations. These activities were included not so much because the author believed in their potency, but because he wanted to satisfy '[t]hose who delight in the terrific, and the horribly sublime' (Pennant-Rea, 2025).

The use of tarot card reading for spiritual and mundane divination emerged in the late eighteenth century. Esoteric tarot is a form of cartomancy, or the interpretation of cards for predicting the future. Some historians consider French occultist Jean-Baptiste Alliette (under the pseudonym Etteilla, a palindrome of his surname) to be the first person to promote using tarotism for divination and to make it a profession. Tarot cards had previously been used for card games, originating early in the fifteenth century in southern Europe. Deployed for divination, tarot practice involves shuffling the card deck, laying them out according to certain rules and making a 'reading' or interpretation based on the symbolism shown on each card and their relationship with each other. Alliette founded an organisation devoted to the study of esoteric tarot and published his own tarot deck that brought together ideas from astrology and the ancient Egyptian mystical text *The Book of Thoth* for divination purposes. His card deck became popular in Paris during the French Revolution as a way for people to predict the fate of France in turbulent times (Decker & Dummett, 2013; Farley, 2009).

By the late nineteenth century, esoteric tarotism had been incorporated into the Occult Revival in England, spurred on by the activities of the Hermetic Order of the Golden Dawn, a secret society established of magicians and diviners from across the social classes who incorporated ideas from the early modern Hermetic Tradition into the symbolism of the card decks. A member of this group, Arthur Edward Waite, designed the Rider-Waite deck to facilitate divination, eventually becoming the most popular deck in the history of tarot. At this stage of development of esoteric tarot, it was viewed as a powerful, mystical experience that should only be practised by those who had been initiated into its occult meaning (Decker & Dummett, 2013; Farley, 2009).

Beyond members of these kinds of secret societies, historians have identified significant changes in how the privileged, well-educated classes in Britain engaged with lay futuring practices during the nineteenth century. Thomas Waters (2015) found that while there was a time (from the 1820s to the 1860s) in which the middle class 'respectable' society rejected superstition, witchcraft and magical beliefs as heathen, scientifically ignorant and the domain of the ill-educated proletarian, by the late Victorian period beliefs about the occult and the supernatural became accepted either as folklore or the basis for 'psychical science' inquiries. Spiritualism, in particular, became popular as a way of conceptualising the afterlife, ghostly hauntings and communicating with the dead. Professional fortune tellers and astrologers became respectable again into the early 1900s. Waters argues, therefore, that there is evidence in British educated society in the Victorian and Edwardian periods of a growing tolerance of magical beliefs and practices.

Andrew Sneddon (2022) similarly shows that in Victorian Ireland, all classes demonstrated strong beliefs in the occult and the supernatural, alongside strong Christian religious faith. The working-class and rural poor continued to believe in fairies, witchcraft, ghosts, death messengers, omens, divination and fortune telling. The educated middle class were interested in astrology, spiritualism and Theosophy and Eastern Mysticism as well as fairy-lore. Some people, including poet William Butler Yeats, joined occult societies in England (including the aforementioned Hermetic Order of the Golden Dawn).

Another example of a well-known individual espousing such beliefs is Sir Arthur Conan Doyle, a physician and the author of the famous Sherlock Holmes detective mysteries. Conan Doyle became a fervent believer in telepathy and spiritualism and in supernatural beings such as fairies and ghosts. He was an active member and later a proselytiser of the British spiritualist movement, attended seances and throughout his lifetime studied psychic phenomena. Living through World War I, for Conan Doyle, was a major impetus in investigating spiritualism, as he attempted to make sense of the great shock the world had undergone and his own grief at the death of his son Kingsley. He wrote several books about spiritualism and viewed himself as a prophet of the future of the world, acting as a medium for an Arabian spirit. Conan Doyle believed that the basis of spiritualism could be proven with the right experimental methods such as the use of photography, therefore trying to bring together Western science and technology with the supernatural and the psychic arts (Homer, 1990).

PALIMPSESTIC TIME, DEEP TIME AND DEEP FUTURES

Social and cultural theorists are beginning to grapple with the notion of chronodiversity as it extends into deep timescapes, and to consider how this idea can influence how we might conceptualise futures. Archaeologists have always relied on material artefacts and features of place and space across millennia to develop their understandings of past cultures. Some archaeologists have begun to use the term 'palimpsestic time'. This term metaphorically uses the material culture term 'palimpsest', which refers to a manuscript or piece of writing on which other inscriptions have been superimposed, but which still bears visible traces of the earlier writing. Older and newer writing can therefore be viewed on the same document simultaneously. Palimpsest has also been used to refer to other forms of material culture, such as buildings, archaeological artefacts or reworked paintings. As such, palimpsestic analysis can adopt a sociocultural perspective in examining the entanglements of materials with social relations in meaning-making practices across time periods (Colwell, 2022).

In his work on palimpsestic time, anthropological archaeologist Geoff Bailey (2007) introduced the notion of time perspectivism: meaning that individuals' temporal, cultural and biographical positioning create different concepts of time. Bailey positions palimpsests as universal features of the material world that can be used by archaeologists to address questions about time perspectivism. He sees material artefacts as combining with other forms of engagement with the past, such as memories, storytelling and dreams, to contribute to temporal relativism. For Bailey, this approach disrupts standard archaeological approaches to time, as well as conventional understandings of past, present and future. He uses material artefacts and sites to probe time perspectivism, noting that one version of palimpsest – palimpsests of meaning – refer to the layers of cultural meaning that have built up in relation to an object or site over time. One example he provides is Stonehenge, which is not only a Neolithic and Bronze Age monument bearing spiritual meaning, but also one taking on different significance from the Iron Age to the current era and beyond. In modern times, Stonehenge retains spiritual meaning for some people (for example, neo-pagans who come there to mark the solstices) but others engage with its historical, heritage and archaeological significance, or appreciate its commercial value as a landmark attracting tourism.

For Caribbean American scholar M Jacqui Alexander, palimpsestic time involves complex layering of temporal fluidities in which the past is continually emerging through to inform the present. Alexander develops a critique of the linearity of time in Western thought by introducing traditional Caribbean spiritual ideas of temporality (Alexander, 2006). Other scholars have evoked the palimpsest metaphor to consider how layered materialities can be used to prompt creative imaginings of futures. For example, anthropologist Alexandrine Boudreault-Fournier (2021) used the left-behind building rubble in Santiago de Cuba and Havana, Cuba, to sense and imagine new presents and possible futures by considering how the present blends into the past.

Some environmental philosophers have argued that due to the dominance of clock time, people acculturated into Western concepts of temporality have difficulty in coming to terms with the risks posed by slow-moving ecological crises. Clocks work well to help people coordinate the hours and minutes in their days, but can do little to help them fully understand the long-term impacts of the environmental devastation that is facing the planet. By pointing out how an object such as a mechanical clock can have such a structuring influence on experiences of temporality, these analyses highlight the sociomateriality and relativity of time. Clocks demonstrate time is passing, and delineate 'before' and 'after' in distinctive ways, helping people to notice change at a daily level. But in so doing, clock time also defines the very notion of 'change'. As Michelle Bastian (2012) points out, simply observing the time on a clock reveals little about what is happening in terms of the melting of the glaciers and ice shelves, the accumulation of greenhouse gases in the atmosphere or the plastics in waterways. She suggests using an indicator of temporality from patterns in nature to predict future impacts of climate change: for example, 'telling time with turtles' by observing long-term patterns in their behaviours.

There are various ways to notice time that involve far longer timescapes. In Western science, the disciplines of geology and palaeontology have always focused on deep time scales, reaching far back into Earth's history to examine how the rocks, minerals and sediments that make up our planet have formed over millions of years, and how the remnants of living creatures have been preserved in the fossil record. Some palaeontologists have already begun to think about what future fossils may look like, particularly as humans continue to make and discard objects such as clothing, tin cans, plastic and concrete items and digital devices which often are abandoned in landfills, left buried in soil and sediment. Such objects, which do not readily degrade organically, can potentially transform into fossils over long periods of time, gradually merging into rock or sedimentary layers. For palaeontologists Sarah Gabbott and Jan Zalasiewicz (2025), these items can be characterised as 'technofossils': humans' ultimate legacy due to the likelihood of their persistence in geological formations.

History of philosophy scholars have engaged with fossils as a way to think about futures using geological insights, engaging with a field of inquiry dubbed 'historical futures' (The Lifetimes Research Collective, 2022). This field seeks to identify the transitional relationships between understandings of the past and address new modes of configuring how pasts relate to anticipated futures. From this perspective, the past and futures are intertwined, so that considering the future involves re-examining and rewriting the past, giving it new meaning, and vice versa. It is argued that 'our concept of the past derives from our ideas about the future; without a concept of the future, history as we know it is not possible' (Simon & Tamm, 2021, p. 7). Moreover, scholars working on historical futures acknowledge the more-than-human dimensions of futures that go beyond the traditional textual sources on which historians have relied: particularly in relation to novel technologies and anthropogenic environmental and climate transformations (Simon & Tamm, 2021).

As one example of this approach, as part of the 'geological turn' in the humanities, the Lifetimes Research Collective, a group based at the University of Oslo, has developed a theory of fossils and fossilisation to rethink the concept of historical futures as part of a new approach to historiography and historical theory. They build on the insights offered by more-than-human theorists such as Barad, Haraway and Bennett (Chapter 1), to argue that considering the sociomaterialities of the landscape as part of decentring the human is integral to historical futures scholarship: or what these researchers term 'geo-materialistic historiographies' (The Lifetimes Research Collective, 2022, p. 6). The project considers what it might mean to investigate futures not as phenomena that are immaterial and accelerating, but instead as outcomes of something slowing down, settling like sediment, calcifying or petrifying.

Using fossilisation, these researchers argue that this move radically challenges historians' concepts of change and continuity, inviting them to engage with deep historical futures. Fossilisation presupposes continuity as it preserves elements of the present into the future, but it also involves radical change, as these materials are transformed through the process from organic to inorganic matter. Positioning objects such as fossils as 'storied matter' that accrue relationships to other things, forces and beings throughout their lifetime (The Lifetimes Research Collective, 2022, p. 21), the Lifetimes Research Collective suggest that speculating about what future fossils may be, and how future palaeontologists who discover them may interpret the past and the present based on the characteristics of the fossils, is an entry point into far futures thinking. Asking what elements of the present will fossilise into the future – thinking with fossilisation – can help us open up temporal imaginations by both considering the deep pasts of fossils and how continuing processes of fossilisation can help rethink our own near or deep futures.

Such a perspective involves a reaching forward of deep time into the future: what may be considered to be 'deep future'. Indeed, this is a term used by anthropologist Vincent Ialenti in his book *Deep Time Reckoning* (Ialenti, 2020), where he reflects on how his fieldwork with nuclear waste experts in Finland helped him adopt such a deep time perspective on the future: or what he calls 'far-future worlds' (Ialenti, 2020, p. xiv). For these experts, assessing the length of time for radioactive nuclear waste in an underground facility to remain dangerous involves timescales of tens of thousands of years. Such evaluations can help identify recurring patterns based on geological, hydrological, ecological and social factors in the past and how these may influence the radioactivity degradation to create scenarios of 'far-future Finlands' (Ialenti, 2020, p. xv). Ialenti argues that pattern thinking (see Chapter 1) is key to identifying the characteristics of far-future worlds. He describes this approach as reckoning with time.

It is important, however, that efforts to engage in deep futures thinking do not distract from near-present future thinking. Bastian (2024) criticised what she characterises as 'chronowashing' in long-term thinking related to environmental crises. An example is the Clock of the

Long Now project founded by the Big Tech entrepreneur Jeff Bezos, one of the wealthiest men in the world. This project involves a clock that uses years, centuries and millennia as its temporal markers in the effort to move thinking beyond conventional clock time. Bastian argues that this mode of thinking has tended to be used in the service of distracting from a focus on the current impacts of extractivist capitalism rather than challenging the socioeconomic inequalities that are already exposing many people to environmental hazards in the present day. It is a way of delaying action and displacing current impacts into the long-term future, allowing privileged social groups and wealthy corporations such as Bezos's Amazon to continue to indulge in these vanity projects simultaneously with their profit-driven activities that damage the environment. For Bastian, moving away from Western notions of linear and clock time should involve thinking of time as relational and political: acknowledging that for marginalised, disadvantaged groups, the climate crisis has already been experienced. As discussed in Chapters 3 and 4, the present-day living conditions of such groups, and their apparent lack of access to positive futures, are often excluded from the visions of the future imagined by those in positions of power and privilege.

REFERENCES

Adam, B. (2003). Reflexive modernization temporalized. *Theory, Culture & Society*, 20(2), 59–78.

Adam, B. (2005). *Timescapes of modernity: The environment and invisible hazards*. Routledge.

Alexander, M. J. (2006). *Pedagogies of crossing: Meditations on feminism, sexual politics, memory, and the sacred*. Duke University Press.

Bailey, G. (2007). Time perspectives, palimpsests and the archaeology of time. *Journal of Anthropological Archaeology*, 26(2), 198–223.

Bastian, M. (2012). Fatally confused: Telling the time in the midst of ecological crises. *Environmental Philosophy*, 9(1), 23–48.
Bastian, M. (2024). Is long-term thinking a trap?: Chronowashing, temporal narcissism, and the time machines of racism. *Environmental Humanities*, 16(2), 403–421.
Beerden, K. (2014). Ancient Greek futures: Diminishing uncertainties by means of divination. *Futures*, 60, 23–29.
Beinorius, A. (2017). Tracing the will of the stars: Indian astrology and divination about natural disasters and threats. In G. J. Schenk (Ed.), *Historical disaster experiences: Towards a comparative and transcultural history of disasters across Asia and Europe* (pp. 225–239). Springer International Publishing.
Bell, K. (2007). Breaking modernity's spell – magic and modern history. *Cultural and Social History*, 4(1), 115–122.
Bell, K. (2012). *The magical imagination: Magic and modernity in urban England, 1780–1914*. Cambridge University Press.
Béres, L. (2012). A thin place: Narratives of space and place, Celtic spirituality and meaning. *Journal of Religion & Spirituality in Social Work: Social Thought*, 31(4), 394–413.
Bever, E. (2008). *The realities of witchcraft and popular magic in early modern europe: Culture, cognition and everyday life*. Springer.
Boschung, D., & Bremme, J. (Eds.). (2015). *The materiality of magic*. Wilhelm Fink.
Boudreault-Fournier, A. (2021). Intimating the possible collapse of the future: Digging into Cuban palimpsests through innovative methodologies. In M. Kazubowski-Houston & M. Auslander (Eds.), *In search of lost futures: Anthropological explorations in multimodality, deep interdisciplinarity, and autoethnography* (pp. 227–253). Springer International Publishing.
Braekman, W. L. (1980). Fortune-telling by the casting of dice: A middle English poem and its background. *Studia Neophilologica*, 52(1), 3–29.
Brendecke, A., & Vogt, P. (Eds.). (2017). *The end of Fortuna and the rise of modernity*. Walter de Gruyter.
Carey, H. M. (2010). Astrology in the Middle Ages. *History Compass*, 8(8), 888–902.
Clucas, S. (2006). *John Dee: Interdisciplinary studies in English renaissance thought*. Springer.
Colwell, C. (2022). A palimpsest theory of objects. *Current Anthropology*, 63(2), 129–157.

Daneshmand, P. (2022). Extispicy and consensus decision-making in ancient Mesopotamia. *DABIR*, *9*(1), 67–85.

Decker, R., & Dummett, M. (2013). *The history of the occult tarot*. Prelude Books.

Driediger-Murphy, L. G. (2019). *Roman Republican augury: Freedom and control*. Oxford University Press.

Driediger-Murphy, L. G., & Eidinow, E. (2019). Introduction. In L. G. Driediger-Murphy & E. Eidinow (Eds.), *Ancient divination and experience*. Oxford University Press.

Dukes, H. (2025). Signs and wonders: Celestial phenomena in 16th-century Germany. *The Public Domain Review*. https://publicdomainreview.org/collection/celestial-phenomena-16th-century-germany/

Farley, H. (2009). *A cultural history of tarot: From entertainment to esotericism*. Bloomsbury Publishing.

Ferkiss, V. (1975). Christianity and the fear of the future. *Zygon*, *10*(3), 250–262.

Gabbott, S., & Zalasiewicz, J. (2025). *Discarded: How technofossils will be our ultimate legacy*. Oxford University Press.

Hacking, I. (1990). *The taming of chance*. Cambridge University Press.

Hartnell, J. (2018). *Medieval bodies: Life, death and art in the Middle Ages*. Profile Books.

Healy-Musson, C. (2019). Thin place: New modes of environmental knowing through contemporary curatorial practice. In G. Feola, H. Geoghegan, & A. Arnall (Eds.), *Climate and culture: Multidisciplinary perspectives on a warming world* (pp. 93–114). Cambridge University Press.

Heiduk, M. (2022). Signs from the afterlife: Consulting the dead about the future in medieval times. In K. Herbers & H.-C. Lehner (Eds.), *Dreams, nature, and practices as signs of the future in the Middle Ages* (pp. 206–231). Brill.

Hoffman, J. (2013). China's search for the future: A genealogical approach. *Futures*, *54*, 53–67.

Homer, M. W. (1990). Sir Arthur Conan Doyle: spiritualism and "New Religions. *Dialogue: A Journal of Mormon Thought*, *23*(4), 97–121.

Ialenti, V. (2020). *Deep time reckoning: How future thinking can help earth now*. MIT Press.

Jeffers, A. (2007). Magic and divination in Ancient Israel. *Religion Compass*, *1*(6), 628–642.

Kentarō, S. (1995). Divination in contemporary Japan: a general overview and an analysis of survey results. *Japanese Journal of Religious Studies*, 22(3/4), 249–266.

Lupton, D. (2012). *Medicine as culture: Illness, disease and the body* (3rd ed.). Sage.

Meylan, N. (2014). Fate is a hero's best friend: towards a socio-political definition of fate in medieval Icelandic literature. *Viking and Medieval Scandinavia*, *10*, 155–172.

North, M. J. (2015). A Mongolian manual of astrology and divination. *The Public Domain Review*. https://publicdomainreview.org/essay/a-mongolian-manual-of-astrology-and-divination/

O'Sullivan, A. (2017). Magic in early medieval Ireland. *Ulster Journal of Archaeology*, 74, 107–117.

Páez, M. M. (2024). Towards an anthropology of destiny: The dynamics of fate in Old Norse literature as illustrated by Vǫlsunga saga. *Gripla*, *35*, 247–278.

Pennant-Rea, N. (2025). The astrologer of the nineteenth century (1825). *The Public Domain Review*. https://publicdomainreview.org/collection/the-astrologer-of-the-nineteenth-century-1825/

Pooley, W. G. (2024). Doubt and the dislocation of magic: France, 1790–1940. *Past & Present*, *262*(1), 133–167.

Simon, Z. B., & Tamm, M. (2021). Historical futures. *History and Theory*, *60*(1), 3–22.

Sneddon, A. (2019). Witchcraft belief, representation and memory in modern Ireland. *Cultural and Social History*, *16*(3), 251–270.

Sneddon, A. (2022). Gender, folklore and magical healing in Ireland, 1852–1922. In J. Atawal, C. Breathnach, & B. Sarah-Anne (Eds.), *Gender and history* (pp. 104–116). Routledge India.

Stiles, A. (2019). Making sense of chaos: civil war, dynasties, and family trees. In L. G. Driediger-Murphy & E. Eidinow (Eds.), *Ancient divination and experience* (134–153). Oxford University Press.

Strådal, S. Ö. (2016). A closer look at the Zodiac and Phlebotomy Men in Wellcome MS 8004. *Mittelalter. Interdisziplinäre Forschung und Rezeptionsgeschichte*, *11*. https://mittelalter.hypotheses.org/8919

Szönyi, G. E. (2014). The hermetic revival in Italy. In C. Partridge (Ed.), *The occult world* (pp. 51–73). Routledge.

The Lifetimes Research Collective (2022). Fossilization, or the matter of historical futures. *History and Theory*, *61*(1), 4–26.

Thomas, E. (2025). Spatializing time: How the long nineteenth century turned time into a line. In N. Emery (Ed.), *The Routledge companion to philosophy of time* (pp. 87–98). Routledge.
Thomas, K. (1973). *Religion and the decline of magic*. Penguin.
Thomas, K. (1984). *Man and the natural world: Changing attitudes in England 1500-1800*. Penguin UK.
Voss, A. (2014). Scrying. In C. Partridge (Ed.), *The occult world* (pp. 580–591). Routledge.
Waters, T. (2015). Magic and the British middle classes, 1750–1900. *Journal of British Studies*, 54(3), 632–653.
Wee, J. Z. (2015). Discovery of the Zodiac Man in cuneiform. *Journal of Cuneiform Studies*, 67(1), 217–233.
Zhang, S. (2018). The heritage practices in a Chinese historic neighbourhood: The manifestation of traditional Feng Shui in Langzhong, China. *International Journal of Heritage Studies*, 24(5), 531–546.
Zongli, L. (2022). Handbook of divination and prognostication in China. Part One: Introduction to the Field. *Chinese Literature, Essays, Articles, Reviews*, 44, 301–307.
Zuesse, E. M. (1975). Divination and deity in African religions. *History of Religions*, 15(2), 158–182.

3

ANTHROPOLOGY AND FUTURES

ANTHROPOLOGY OF TEMPORALITIES

While anthropologists have argued that their discipline has neglected the future as a subject of inquiry, it is also evident that they have long been fascinated by how non-Western cultures conceptualise temporality and engage in customs and traditions of futures thinking. Anthropological investigations into concepts and practices of time have identified the diversity across cultures of human experiences of time and have also considered the theoretical dimensions of temporalities. A 1992 review of the literature on the cultural anthropology of time written by Nancy Munn (1992) opened with her remarks about the complexity and ever-growing body of research, such that it is a difficult topic about which to provide a coherent overview. She further pointed out that time cannot be considered without acknowledging space, and that the two phenomena cannot be disentangled, yet anthropologists have often not considered these entanglements.

Munn (1992) observed that in the symbolic interactionist scholarship of Emile Durkheim (a foundational scholar in both anthropology and sociology), personal awareness of time passing was differentiated from collective understandings of time, which relied on a large extent on social or religious rituals serving to differentiate between 'profane' or 'sacred' time. Another early anthropologist, Bronislaw Malinowsky, adopted a functionalist

DOI: 10.4324/9781003726579-3

perspective, using the concept of 'time-reckoning' as a means of coordinating social activities, dating events and gauging the length of temporal spans. For his part, in his influential scholarship Edward Evan Evans-Pritchard adopted the notion of 'oecological time', portraying the passage of time as perceived through the lens of cultural concepts together with observations of the rhythms and cycles of the natural world. Experiences of time for Evans-Pritchard were therefore processual and dynamic but also structured through practices and understandings passed on through generations in a particular culture.

Bringing these and a number of other anthropologists' theories together, Munn (1992) concluded that human temporality is a symbolic process that is configured through quotidian experiences. The multiple dimensions of time are understood or experienced though meaningful interrelationships with people, things and place. For Munn, the past-present-future relation is always part of these experiences: lived presents are always infused with pasts and futures. This approach is therefore a sociomaterial as well as a phenomenological perspective on time, recognising the intertwining of cultural concepts of time with the biological rhythms of human bodies and the environments in which they live. Through habit, routine and acculturation, these experiences of time can operate at the subconscious level of perception.

Alfred Gell is another influential scholar of the anthropology of time. His book of that title (Gell, 1992) identified four main approaches in time research: developmental psychology, symbolic anthropology, economic theories of time and phenomenological theories. Gell went on to present his own model of social/cognitive time in this book. In later writing, however, Gell (1998) had rethought his position on how best to approach the anthropology of time. He called for anthropological scholarship that focused less on the ways that the concept of time is socially and culturally determined, and more on how what he refers to as 'temporal relations' and practices of 'time-use' and 'time-talk' are variable across societies and cultures. He was highly critical of anthropological scholarship that positioned 'the Other' as having a different understanding of time from 'Us'. In the interests of departing from this simplistic binary opposition, Gell advocated for anthropologists of time to engage more fully with the scholarship of Pierre Bourdieu on temporal experience and attitudes in specific cultural settings. For Gell, Bourdieu's ethnographic insights on the experience of 'pastness in the present' and 'futurity in the present' offered more complex understandings of temporal experience that did not make binary distinctions between cyclical and linear time. Such an approach instead recognises the ways that evolving past-present-future temporal experiences are structured in all cultures by natural and acculturated schedules such as the ordering of the months, feasts and fast-days, and periods of labour and relaxation.

In later anthropological scholarship, researchers have investigated field sites in the Global North in terms of how people conceptualise time, including futures. One example is Felix Ringel's (2016) ethnography of what he calls 'Germany's fastest shrinking city', which appears to have little future – Hoyerswerda, in post-socialist East Germany. His fieldwork identified how post-socialist visions of the future rely on unrealistic fantasies of radical transformation and improvements in people's living conditions, while understandings of their present-day experiences are fixated on the past. Neither perspective fully addresses the long-term repercussions of German reunification, or the intersections between remembrance or forgetting of past experiences and their expectations of the yet-to-come. Ringel's field work demonstrated that the ways that people relate to the future are not fixed and stable, and that temporalities cannot be said to be discrete or have inherent qualities. Instead, they are contingent and unstable, evolving in and reproduced by everyday practices, structured through social, economic and political currents that are localised. He therefore advocated for anthropologies of time that are 'presentist' explorations of the roles that time is made to play in the present.

In another example that links religious beliefs to temporal experiences, anthropologists Michal Kravel-Tovi and Yoram Bilu (2008) set out to discover how messianists among the Jewish ultraorthodox Chabad (Lubavitch) Hasidic sect employed temporal categories to deal with the crisis entailed in the death of their spiritual leader and expected Messiah, Rabbe Menachem Mendel Schneerson. Their fieldwork with members of this community at the building in which they meet in New York City found that the failure of this prophecy was managed through 'timework' involving the development of an elaborate ritual system composed of linguistic and embodied practices designed to make the absent Rebbe feel present and still alive and well. These rituals, which include placing the Rebbe's empty chair front and centre and suggesting his spiritual presence inhabits it as well as the screening of video recordings of his talks, constitute a present experienced as flowing from and identical with the past. The rituals created at this site also operate to blur the boundary between the present and the future, with continuing discussions about how the coming redemption could occur at any moment. Through these practices and beliefs, the death of the expected Messiah was dealt with by presenting it as a trial of faith rather than an excruciating reality, maintaining the illusion of the possibility of redemption.

ANTHROPOLOGY OF THE FUTURE AND FUTURES ANTHROPOLOGY

A distinctive anthropology of the future has only recently emerged. Rebecca Bryant and Daniel Knight's *The Anthropology of the Future* (2019) is one of the key books on this topic. Each chapter covers a specific cultural concept related to the future: anticipation, expectation, speculation, potentiality, hope and destiny. This structuring emphasises the sociocultural dimensions of futures thinking. Bryant and Knight begin the book with thoughts about how the discipline of anthropology has addressed scholarly inquiry into the topic of the future and identify a reorientation in the twenty-first century. They call for anthropological research about the future that is rooted in the collective materialities and shared meanings and practices of everyday life. They also suggest that the conservative tendency of anthropological research focused on futures to call for a return to traditions of the past or to legitimise the present day should be resisted. Bryant and Knight adopt a more radical perspective, noting that the present is characterised by clashes between the imperatives of the 'time-reckoning of capitalism' (Bryant & Knight, 2019, p. 13), everyday experiences of time and secular and religious temporalities.

Bryant and Knight refer to the 'thickening and thinning of temporal horizons' (Bryant & Knight, 2019, p. 14) as a dominant theme of their book, including the ways that people, either individually or collectively, attempt to 'trick time' by modifying or distorting the structures of time in which they are sited. Another theme in their book is that of shared 'timespaces', and the question of how people move through their lives in these timespaces. Timespaces are sociomaterial phenomena, involving embodied experience, memories and accultured traditions coming together to give meaning to a physical environment. For Bryant and Knight's argument, time is positioned as inherently teleological. What they mean by this is that as part of the practices and customs of everyday life, temporality is reproduced in open-ended, indeterminate ways that serve a purpose. The thickening and thinning of temporalities occur dynamically at these moments. In some situations, the future may seem to be almost present, as in times of political conflict, natural catastrophe or social turmoil, when 'the unknown may come right to one's door' (Bryant & Knight, 2019, p. 19). At other times, a threat may seem more distant and difficult to know. They argue that the most productive way to engage in anthropological inquiry is to orient oneself to temporal teleologies of the actions of everyday life, by observing and documenting it.

Several anthropologists have in recent times developed a subfield of research that they term 'futures anthropology' (Kazubowski-Houston & Auslander, 2021; Pink & Salazar, 2020; Pink et al., 2024; Salazar et al., 2017). Such initiatives push anthropology beyond a focus on social practices in non-Western cultures and inquire into how more hopeful futures might be imagined in an era which is characterised by polycrises. These scholars argue for an approach to futures that examines how they are constituted and imagined as part of the everyday and with and through people's embodied and experiential knowledge, including those who engage in futures thinking as part of their work. Futures anthropology uses ethnographic methods to understand the ways in which sociotechnical imaginaries are responded to in mundane practices of living. Researchers call for a renewed anthropological inquiry which investigates challenged and contested futures using speculative and creative approaches. There is a strong focus on offering ideas about alternative futures and to intervene in world-making activities rather than simply documenting them. Researchers emphasise the emergent and continent nature of future imaginaries as they are incorporated into everyday lives, including strategies of adoption, improvisation, resistance or rejection.

Many of these ideas were outlined in the 'Futures Anthropologies Manifesto' developed at the 2014 conference of the European Association of Social Anthropology by members of the futures anthropologies network (EASA Future Anthropologies Network, 2017). The manifesto argues for anthropologists to confront and intervene in the challenges of contested, complex and controversial futures, and to de-centre the human in doing so. It describes futures as plural, dynamic and non-linear and the anthropology of the future as building on traditions and reflecting on pasts. It supports an ethics of responsibility and care, a politics of listening, telling imaginative stories and creating and designing materials and processes to provoke and disrupt ideas of futures.

For Sarah Pink (2025) acknowledging the affective and emplaced dimensions of futures is a key focus of futures anthropology. In her scholarship, she considers the questions of the affective dimensions of futures: how futures feel to people, and which will feel right. Pink argues that trust, as an anticipatory concept involving feelings of familiarity and confidence, is particularly important to understand. Unless a vision of a possible future is viewed with trust, people will lack confidence in it. Pink characterises both trust and futures as always emerging, contingent, uncertain and emplaced. Providing examples from her ethnographic research with Australians about their use of home energy use and automated technologies, Pink shows that place is fundamental to participants' feelings about these technologies in the present and their imaginaries of future use. The trusted futures that people wished to work towards for these technologies were built on people's familiarity with their domestic and geographical setting, their relationships with other people nearby, the local weather conditions or emergencies with which they had had experience over time, and their expectations about changes in the climate or extreme weather events in the future.

Futures anthropology researchers are also interested in conducting fieldwork in the sites where futures are made and discussed by experts or lay people. This scholarship involves critical analysis of social imaginaries presented in industry reports about new technologies, or interviews and ethnographic observations of professionals such as the CEOs of technology advocacy groups, promoters and developers of new commodities and services and others engaged in leadership and decision-making in the workplace, to discern how they express their views, experiences and imaginaries about the future. These sites have been described as constituting a 'mid-level futures space', where people are sourcing or delivering knowledge about the future or facilitating their own or work colleagues' futures-focused decision-making. In this often-neglected space, people are actively engaging with futures as a quotidian practice. However, they are doing so in a context in which it is an integral part of work practices, where the hype about novel technologies or services must be continually negotiated in the context of complex organisations and socioeconomic structures (Pink et al., 2024).

ANTHROPOLOGIES OF MAGIC AND DIVINATION

Early anthropologists devoted attention to magical practices and belief systems among the small-scale cultures with which they conducted ethnographic fieldwork. Marcel Mauss' book *A General Theory of Magic* (2005) drew on ethnographies across a number of cultures, including contemporary Western societies, to present a tripartite cross-cultural theory of magical practice and belief systems. According to Mauss, magic is a social phenomenon, involving performances of gestures and words that seek to make change by indeterminate or invisible means. These actions are symbolic, collectively imagined and recognised in specific cultural contexts. Mauss argued that all magic involves the combination of three elements: magician, magical representation and magical rite. A magician (the agent who performs magic) has certain qualities, skills or authority that others do not possess. Magicians use certain representations (such as the utterance of spells or evoking shared ideas or principles) together with rites to effect magical transformations. These individuals, actions and beliefs are not inherently magical but are agreed to be so through collective belief and customs that people regard as extraordinary. Mauss viewed contemporary Western medicine and science as imbued with magical thinking and prestige due to the out-of-the-ordinary knowledge, authority and power that these professions entail.

Malinowski is another influential example. Building on insights from his fieldwork in Melanesia (1922/1994), Malinowski argued that across the world, what he termed 'magical performances' have three essential aspects: the formula, the rite and the condition of the performer of the ceremonies. Magical performances are therefore sociomaterial phenomena that are contingent on factors such as the cultural and geographic context in which they are carried out, and are continually emergent in response to the conditions at the time. Malinowski viewed magical performances as a way for societies to deal with conditions of unpredictability, unaccountable or mysterious forces and fortunate coincidences in which luck seems to play a major part.

The classic anthropology of divination and fortune telling is Evans-Pritchard's *Witchcraft, Oracles and Magic among the Azande* (1937), bringing together theories of knowledge with that of religion and spirituality. Evans-Pritchard conducted ethnographic research with the Azande, an ethnic group in southern Sudan, Central Africa. Adopting a structural functionalist approach, he suggested that the Azande's lay futuring practices were a way of dealing with potentially harmful conflict within their society. The Azande's beliefs about witchcraft, oracles and magic served to stabilise social relationships and provide explanations for unfortunate events such as deaths, as well as involving a system of vengeance against those deemed to be responsible. Oracles were involved in deciding which person's magic may have led to the death or other misfortune.

Evans-Pritchard and other structural functionalist anthropologists investigating religious and supernatural belief systems at this time viewed such worldviews as rational, socially functional and common to all societies, including those in the West. In other words, they viewed magic and related activities such as divination and fortune telling as 'a human universal' (Wallis, 2017, p. 237). They therefore departed from earlier anthropological inquiries which positioned these belief systems as superstitious and primitive, evidence of less 'civilised' societies (Bryant & Knight, 2019; Kazubowski-Houston & Auslander, 2021).

More recent fieldwork has included ethnographies by anthropologists who themselves have insider perspectives rather than treating the cultures they are studying as 'the exotic other'. One example is American cultural anthropologist Barbara Tedlock (2001, 2006), who herself practiced as a shamanic healer and diviner after being trained and initiated by the K'iche' Maya of highland Guatemala. Tedlock wrote several essays reflecting on the cultural meaning of divination. She defined divinatory inquiry as 'a way of exploring the unknown in order to elicit answers (that is, oracles) to questions beyond the range of ordinary human understanding' (Tedlock, 2001, p. 189). Tedlock (2006) viewed such inquiry as a form of intentional shared social action, involving the practical mastery of diviners. Such a definition could equally be applied to scientific research. Indeed, Tedlock (2006) made the important point that while in post-Enlightenment societies so-called rational science is frequently privileged over the 'superstition' of traditional divination practices, recent physical scientific thought recognises the uncertainties of human sensory observations and commonsense experiences of the material world (for example, quantum theory, discussed in Chapter 1).

Building on her ethnographic work, Tedlock (2001, 2006) found that across contemporary cultures, diviners draw on their expert knowledge of cultural traditions, together with using their insight, intuition and imagination and dialogue with their clients, to interpret signs. They act as mediums or vehicles for divinatory power by linking diverse domains of information, metaphor and symbolism with affective or sensory experience, sometimes using drugs or other forms of embodied transformation to achieve their insights. Tedlock (2006) identified four main types of divination. These are omen (reading natural signs such as the flight of birds); pattern (making a shape or design and then interpreting it using fixed guidelines); symbol (such as card reading or palmistry); and trance (contacting spirits to ask them questions). These divination techniques involve a combination of inductive, interpretative and intuitive techniques and ways of knowing (Tedlock, 2001). As one example, among the Indigenous peoples of the Americas, the narration of myths is combined in divinatory practice with visualisation and embodiment. Diviners may go into trances, communicate with spirits by using substances or manipulating objects such as stones, seeds or bones. K'iche' Maya diviners use hallucinogenic seeds and crystals with narratives that centre interpretation of days on the Indigenous calendar, confessions of the client and a force that runs through the diviner's body to arrive at an understanding of the client's needs (Tedlock, 2001).

In other anthropological inquiry, scholars have considered why lay futuring practices involving omens, oracles and divination are so common across cultures. Pascal Boyer (2020), for example, investigated how divination becomes so persuasive for those who seek it, and why it is required for collective decision-making. Boyer notes that one reason for the prognostications of diviners being accepted as persuasive is that they are considered by others to be less influenced by the diviners' own vested interests or intentions. The information must also be seen to be generated through the process of divination, with the diviner as a medium for it, rather than based on pre-existing knowledge. Thus, it is the objects used that 'speak' for the diviner (for example, tarot cards, dice, bones, crystal ball, lines on a person's palm), while the diviner interprets their meaning. In the case of trance-based divination, it is the spirit or deity that shapes the content of the diviners' utterances. This apparent disinterested stance – or what Boyer describes as 'ostensive detachment' – is important when diviners are relied upon to determine who is responsible for misfortune or which path to take when considering the future. People seeking their advice need to be able to trust the quality and truthfulness of their judgements to help them make decisions based on the information provided.

An analysis of the role of fortune telling among Icelandic women (Kissman, 1990) emphasised the more-than-human relational dimensions of these practices, the social function they play and their connection with traditional customs. In the sparsely populated and isolated island of Iceland, where winters are long, cold and dark and there is an ever-present threat of extreme weather events or volcanic activities, belief in supernatural phenomena dating from pre-Christian Norse religious practices remain among many people. The ritual of fortune telling is an important practice that binds female friendships and supportive networks. While there are professional fortune tellers whose services are sought by both men and women, it is mostly practised by female friends for each other as part of informal social networks. The most common practices are interpreting patterns left by dried coffee liquid in cups, palmistry and readings of playing cards. Conducted in a group setting, these modes of divination work to minimise conflicts and provide social and emotional support in stressful situations, as well as giving people reassurance or advice about alternative choices of action. These lay futuring practices also offer a way to pass on women's folk traditions and beliefs to the next generation.

POLITICAL ECONOMIES OF DIVINATION

Another approach to the anthropology of divination adopts a social structural perspective based on political economy theories. The work of Arjun Appadurai in his book *The Future as Cultural Fact* (2013) is one such example. In this collection of essays, Appadurai focuses on urban slum dwellers in India and their struggle to improve their lives in developing a 'politics of hope'. He notes that it is difficult for people in this situation of deprivation to shape the future, for they have little access to cultural or economic resources to do so. However, Appadurai argues that this politics of hope, together with a collective capacity for imagination, is the key to a revitalised anthropology of the future. He portrays collective imagination as a local initiative in the face of globalisation, requiring contextualised knowledge. Appadurai points out that modern Western approaches to prediction, together with the witchcraft, sorcery and divination practiced in earlier Western eras and across global contemporary societies, are all ways of engaging in anticipation. He contrasts the ethics of possibility with the ethics of probability. The ethics of possibility refers to increasing hope and expanding the imagination among ordinary people, whereas the ethics of probability relates to top-down ways of thinking, feeling and acting based on rationalistic, scientific principles. Where the future is formed is at the juncture of these contrasting modes of futures thinking, as part of dynamic and fluid processes of negotiation and struggle.

This scholarship has been supported by the writings of anthropologists such as Anna Tsing, whose book *The Mushroom at the End of the World: On the Possibility of Life in Capitalist Ruins* (2015) presents a critique of the impacts on the more-than-human world of the logics of late capitalism. Tsing advocates for exploring ways for humans and nonhumans to persevere and flourish in capitalism's environmental ruins. She tells stories about the matsutake, a mushroom that plays a major role in Japanese traditional culture and now bears importance in multiple other geographical regions, including Finland, China, Laos and the USA. Based on Tsing's fieldwork in these sites, her narratives about the matsutake illustrate the connections between this fungus, other living creatures in the ecosystems it inhabits and the humans who gather and consume it. These stories involve descriptions of the devastated landscape in Japan due to industrial exploitation (where this mushroom can flourish even when other species cannot). The matsutake is therefore an example of resilience in the changing environmental conditions around the world.

Configuring these narratives for Tsing is part of what she characterises as the 'arts of noticing', developed by mushroom pickers and foragers when using their senses to locate the prized fungus. Tsing uses these practices as a metaphor for developing a hopeful politics. She argues that humans' survival into an uncertain future requires arts of noticing as well as cultivating (both literally and metaphorically) our collaborative relationships and kinships with other living beings. As Tsing argues, we once knew where we were going – now we have to use our imaginations to find new pathways. She identifies the concept of 'third nature', or 'what manages to live despite capitalism' (such as matsutake mushrooms) (Tsing, 2015, p. iix). This 'third nature' as it is applied to futures thinking might be thought of as a radical way through the constraints of a domain of expertise that has become harnessed to the drives and values of commodity culture and profit-driven enterprise.

Other anthropologists have engaged in fieldwork, exploring the role of other living things in local economies and humans' experiences of futures. For example, Keren Marín González (2025) investigated the relationship between plants and the emergence of future imaginaries by addressing the role of the coca plant (the source of cocaine) in shaping the temporal experiences of coca growers in Sierra de la Macarena, Colombia. Drawing on the concept of affective encounters, Marín González identified coca assemblages and the affective encounters they generate during times of prosperity, war and uncertainty. These encounters involve experiences and interactions between human and non-human beings capable of provoking, unsettling or inspiring changes. This study highlights how the future, both as a temporality and a political project, was reimagined through the affective, economic and prospective affordances that the coca plant offered. During the rise of the coca economy in the decade between 1970 and 1980, in which farmers were encouraged by the Colombian state to grow coco plants, there were three distinct temporal regimes that shaped the everyday lives of the coca growers: revolutionary time, market time and coca's own temporality. During the emergence of the 'war on drugs' (1990–2020), people's anticipations about the future shifted from hope to fear due to a new politics marked by violence and military control. The desires, and possibilities previously sustained by the coca economy were altered as new actors, practices and discourses came into play, impacting intergenerational experiences of time and temporality among the coca growers.

The work of Jean and John Comaroff (1999) on what they term 'occult economies' has been influential in critical anthropologies of late stage capitalism. Focusing on post-colonial South Africa, the Comaroffs define occult economies as 'the deployment, real or imagined, of magical means for material ends' (Comaroff & Comaroff, 1999, p. 279). They see these practices of the mystical arts, including divination and the use of oracles, not as an iteration of or retreat into a more 'traditional', 'superstitious' past, but rather as a retooling of culturally familiar tropes, narratives and customs to meet new objectives. In the case of Black South Africans, these objectives include expressing discontent with modernity, late capitalism and colonisation, and attempting to flourish within these constraints: 'new magic for new situations' (Comaroff & Comaroff, 1999, p. 284). Occult belief systems and practices therefore operate to help Black South Africans make sense of and control the mysterious forces of the neoliberal global economy.

Researchers have explored concepts of fate and fortune in relation to occult economies in other parts of contemporary Africa. A special issue on this topic presented five case studies from Western and Southern Africa, focusing on how notions of luck require certain forms of work to achieve economic objectives (Gaibazzi & Gardini, 2015). The collection investigated practices of agriculture, migration, diamond mining, petty trade and popular television shows. These case studies demonstrate that fate and fortune were heuristic devices, used to help people negotiate the contingent dimensions of economic life and direct the effort required to pursue gainful activities as well as exerting some degree of control over the non-human forces that govern the distribution of wealth in their cultures. For example, one of the articles in this collection explores notions of luck, divine guidance and blessing shared by diamond miners in Sierra Leone (D'Angelo, 2015). A 'vocabulary of contingency' is identified: that is, the terms and notions through which the miners, engaging in a high-risk but potentially lucrative activity, make sense of their successes and failures, including the supernatural forces that determine diamond discoveries. Some miners pray for divine intervention in finding diamonds, while others commission local ritual specialists to communicate with spiritual beings and contribute sacrificial offerings to guide the way to the precious stones. In invoking fate and fortune, the miners promote norms, ethical orientations and practical habits that rely on a continuum of social relations between human and non-human beings, the worldly and the divine.

Crucially, the Comaroffs and others (Moeran & de Waal Malefyt, 2018; Skovgaard-Smith & Hirst, 2023) have pointed out that there are parallels in Western cultures of such belief systems, which frequently present wealth accumulation in late state capitalism as due to the almost magical mysterious workings of the market, together with good luck. A key point made in these analyses of 'magical capitalism' is that magic and modernity have frequently been positioned as opposite to each other, yet the magical remains a central dimension of modernity, including the operation of speculation and market forces in late-stage capitalism. In the face of growing uncertainty and the unknown, the modern world has been re-enchanted with visions of progress, technological advancement and wealth accumulation, where 'rational' and 'irrational' thought systems and forces co-exist (Moeran & de Waal Malefyt, 2018; Skovgaard-Smith & Hirst, 2023).

As shown in Chapter 1, professional divination has a very long history as a form of paid work, stretching over millennia. In her ethnographic study of professional tarot card readers in New York City, Karen Gregory (2019) observed how these 'spiritual workers' feel obliged to engage in certain activities as part of the 'spiritual marketplace'. To achieve success, tarot readers must position themselves as credible diviners who are properly trained, establishing reputation and networks of patronage through word-of-mouth. As internet and digital devices have expanded, the spiritual workplace also requires proficiency in attracting attention and building online networks as part of developing a 'personal brand'.

For other examples of Western magical capitalism assemblages, we only need to look at how the promoters and developers of AI, automated technologies such as self-driving cars and other novel or proposed digital devices and software have continually used the language of magic and enchantment to encourage people to adopt these technologies in the interest of profit-making, even in the absence of proof that these technologies work as promised or imagined (Elish & boyd, 2018; Hanna & Bender, 2024). Self-improvement, entrepreneurial and financial influencers on social media are also key players in Western magical capitalism, treated as gurus by their followers for promising to transform people's lives though the wisdom they offer. Similarly, management consultants who promise to turn around the fortunes of businesses are also often treated as if they possess extraordinary insights and power to make change (Skovgaard-Smith & Hirst, 2023).

The World Economic Forum meeting held each year at Davos, Switzerland, provides a compelling instance of magical capitalism. At this meeting, powerful people gather for a talkfest, including heads of state, billionaires, celebrities and the leaders of global non-government organisations. Future thinking has a prominent role these discussions, couched in corporate-speak and meaningless vague phrases, with performative nods to the importance of improving all people's lives through capitalist economic development. In Davos promotions and media coverage of the event, the participants are portrayed as prophets whose wise and inspirational pronouncements will change the world. In accordance with the theories of magic put forward by Mauss and Malinowski, these people can be viewed as engaged in magical performances and rituals, supported by collective belief systems that imbue these individuals and the event with enchantment and the power to achieve miraculous economic and social transformations (Moeran & de Waal Malefyt, 2018).

DECOLONISING ANTHROPOLOGIES OF THE FUTURE

A recent move in anthropology has called for the decolonising of futures thinking in the attempt to cast off the exoticism that has often characterised these investigations. Engaging with Indigenous techniques of pattern thinking and spiral time (Chapter 1) offers one approach to decolonisation. In the Noongar language of southwest Western Australia, for example, the English phrase 'learning journey' cannot be easily translated. The Noongar term *katitjin bidi* is the closest equivalent. This term encompasses knowing or understanding, travelling along a path but also understanding place-based obligations and responsibilities to care and therefore a commitment to action (Wooltorton et al., 2020). For the Noongar way of thinking, the concept of the 'long now' incorporates the idea that the past and future are always part of the present. Stories, memories and experiences from the past remain central to current ways of being, feeling and seeing. They are often shared with stories that are passed from generation to generation. This approach to knowing and learning incorporates giving and finding meaning using cycles of exploration in four ways: experiential knowing engendered from direct experience; identifying patterns using arts-based methods to reflect on experiences (or creative knowing); transforming these patterns into concepts or language through critical conversations; and taking action based on the knowledge synthesised from these elements coming together. These methods are repeated through cycles, with each cycle building on and enriching the next.

Other researchers have engaged with Australian Indigenous cosmologies by suggesting the idea of Feeling and Hearing Country as a research method (Poelina et al., 2023). A research collective, comprised of Indigenous Australians Anne Poelina, Marlikka Perdrisat and Edwin Lee Mulligan, all from Martuwarra, Kimberley River Country in north-west Australia, and Anglo-Celtic settler Sandra Wooltorton, developed a sensory process of knowing and being based on the Indigenous knowledges of the region. For these researchers, Feeling and Hearing Country is a decolonial participative creative process that links ancestral wisdom to the present while co-creating healthy futures and enlivening the human spirit and the landscapes in which people dwell. It is a way of deepening people's empathy and relationship with Country: particularly those who have been acculturated into an extractivist Western worldview on the natural world. Co-operative inquiry is the foundation for the Feeling and Hearing Country research method. This is a process in which co-researchers engage in iterative action and reflection, involving experiential knowing, presentational forms of knowing, propositional knowing and practical knowing through practising acquired skills. Examples provided by the authors is talking a walk along a river, through bushland or by the beach, using one's embodied senses and arts of noticing to become familiar with the place and the creatures living in it and forming kinship with them. Paying close attention to Country as a living being with which people share reciprocity may involve making records through photography, film, writing or sketching, or responding with artwork, storytelling or music-making.

Writing from the perspective of Africa, Robin Bourgeois, Geci Karuri-Sebina and Kwamou Eva Feukeu (2024) argue for seeing the future as a public good and decolonising the future through participatory action research. For these scholars, colonisation has stolen the futures of those who have been colonised, denying them trajectories that otherwise would have taken place. Coloniality can commodify social imaginaries of the future, exploiting them as a resource just as human bodies have been exploited. To counter this, Bourgeois, Karuri-Sebina and Feukeu suggest moves towards the decolonising of individual and collective imaginations, working to extract colonised Africa from the structures imposed by the colonisers. This involves departing from the narrow understanding of futures that see them as areas of expertise developed by experts from the Global North to be taught to those in the Majority World, thereby imposing Western cultural values and priorities. The authors call for an alternative Afrocentric perspective on future thinking led by participatory action research.

An example of such a participatory practice was identified in a study of how young people of colour across the world create activist stances when engaging in multiplayer video games, centring hope and possibility. They achieve this through hacking, glitching and other modifications of popular video games as a socio-political activity, seeking to organise resistance against racialisation in the games and to work towards new futures for people of colour. A gaming practice in which they engaged was spawning and respawning: instances where a character is made to blend racial/gender positionalities (spawning) or to return to a gaming environment after it has been eliminated or 'killed off' (respawning). Another technique used by the young gamers was to collectively design and negotiate new rules for gameplay that remove violence and racialised aggression and instead highlighted social justice issues, as well as making firewalls to keep out gamers who challenged this socio-political work (Cortez et al., 2022).

In a collaborative decolonial approach to futuring project, Swedish-based researchers worked with South African colleagues to develop a praxis applying traditions from across the African continent together with Western more-than-human theory. They developed the 'Entangled Time Tree' heuristic to acknowledge multiple pasts, diverse presents and alternative ways of conceptualising ecological futures in African cosmologies and how these philosophies and traditions are entangled with other concepts of temporalities (Terry et al., 2024). The research group proposed that diverse forms of African storytelling constitute critically underexplored forms of knowledge that offer distinctive visions and pathways for a decolonial future globally. The heuristic acknowledges and reintroduces multiple lost and erased knowledges and distorted truths from the past. It visually presents time as a baobab tree with deep roots in the past, referencing the ancestors, and rhizomes that represent the entangled nature of knowledge and materiality. The tree branches inform multiple presents from which futures extend. The heuristic also incorporates images portraying fractal and pattern thinking from African and other cosmologies to offer alternatives to Western hegemonic time. One of the African concepts they incorporate in their heuristic is Sankofa (an Akan term meaning 'to go back and get it'). A symbol for Sankofa shows a mythical bird flying forward with its head turned backward. The bird carries an egg in its mouth, representing knowledge of the past upon which wisdom is based and signifying the generation to come that would benefit from that wisdom.

Working with Zapotec communities in southern Mexico, Paola Velasco-Herrejón, Thomas Bauwens and Martin Calisto Friant (2022) sought to identify how their Indigenous worldviews compared with modernist Western visions of sustainability in the context of the energy transition to renewable sources. The researchers conducted interviews, focus groups and participant observation with people living in these communities. They showed that their Indigenous worldviews often clashed with dominant Western visions of what should be achieved. The concept of *comunalidad*, central to Zapotec cultural identity, was expressed. This concept is founded in the struggles in which the Indigenous people have confronted colonialism, including holding on to their right to natural resources and to self-determination. *Comunalidad* emphasises the importance of a strong relationship of survival and protection between humans and the natural world. It is governed by the principles of collaborative forms of work, mutual respect for others, and reciprocity between people, communities and ecosystems. This worldview comes into conflict with Western ideas about introducing wind farms to generate sustainable electricity, which have an impact on wildlife, particularly birds and bats. The wind farm industry also does not recognise the communal approach to land held by the Zapotec people and the importance of communal decision-making. The authors therefore suggest that efforts to develop sustainable energy in regions such as those occupied by the Zapotec will not be successful or socially just if their viewpoints are not acknowledged.

Decolonialisation of futures cannot be easily achieved when societies or nations are forced to live under conditions of continuing colonisation or armed conflict. In these conditions, the future may be considered as a phenomenon that cannot easily be imagined in positive terms. This is a point made by contributors to a special journal issue on Palestinian futures (Joronen et al., 2021). For Palestinians, their future is tied to prolonged debates about 'conflict resolution'. These discussions involve plans and proposals made on their behalf by international organisations who have imposed 'solutions' on Palestinians for the uncertainty, violence and conflict to which they have been exposed for decades as part of contestations over the territory they occupy. Such negotiations, accords or agreements outline a future for Palestinians as a geopolitical performance, where the language of peace and reconciliation fails to have a material impact on the ongoing conditions of colonialisation and dispossession. In this situation, the future for Palestinians seems to offer only more conflict and colonial violence. As a consequence, 'the Palestine future is "suffocated", made intolerable' (Joronen et al., 2021, p. 278).

SPECULATIVE AND HAUNTOLOGICAL ANTHROPOLOGIES OF FUTURES

Some anthropologists have engaged with speculative fiction woven through narratives from their fieldwork as a way of contributing to futures anthropology. One example is Roanne van Voorst (2024), who has developed the idea of 'anthropological fiction'. For van Voorst, anthropological fiction provides a way for anthropologists to develop rich narratives from ethnographic work that goes beyond traditional documentation of belief systems and customs in a field site. In her anthropological writing, she creates fictional narratives that are set within the familiar structures of academic ethnographic accounts, crafted to create alternative plausible futures within the existing sociomaterial setting of the field site. The use of fiction for van Voorst provides an opportunity to employ anthropology as a speculative art to promote innovative thinking and compelling storytelling. Rather than crafting narratives that imagine completely different worlds, van Voorst is inspired by anthropologists such as Anna Tsing to build on her ethnographic findings in ways that encourage readers to identify with these envisaged futures. For instance, she has used insights from her field work with people who adopt an ethical vegan stance to create a near-future narrative where plant-eating is the norm and animals are no longer slaughtered for food.

In his work, Juan Francisco Salazar (2017) brings together futures anthropology, more-than-human concepts and Haraway's approach to speculative fabulation in the context of Antarctica. Salazar conducted fieldwork with transient communities in Antarctica to understand how people living there imagined and explained how the future of the Antarctic is unfolding at a time in which human engagement with and habitation of the continent is increasing through scientific and tourism activities and global warming is changing its ecosystems. This research positioned Antarctica as a more-than-human geographical entity that is shaping the future of the planet and as a laboratory not only for environmental science but also for thinking through different ways of living and being in the context of the climate crisis. After four years of summer season fieldwork in the Antarctic Peninsula, Salazar presented his ethnographic findings in a film, *Nightfall on Gaia*, a speculative documentary that positions the futures of extreme environments such as those in Antarctica as deeply relational and immanent to the present. The film's plot features a fictional character in the year 2043, interspersed with footage from Salazar's fieldwork with the communities with which he engaged, including scientists, military, medical, logistics and educator personnel, and tourist and tourism operators. He describes his speculative documentary as a creative account of possibility, embodying 'as if', 'not as yet' and 'about to be' futures. This is a radical departure from the traditional anthropological documentary film, which has sought to provide a 'realistic' account of past and present traditions and customs in a specific cultural context.

Johannes Sjöberg (2020) has similarly experimented with combining anthropological ethnographic methods with science fiction and filmmaking in his research with English youth about environmental threats. He calls this approach 'ethno science fiction', a co-created genre of ethnographic film in which research participants express their imagined futures through projective improvisation. Part of this project involved making science fiction films with his research participants, who lived in regions of England that had been drastically affected by environmental change: for example, major flooding and land clearing to make way for building developments. The films drew on these young people's past and present experiences of these transformations in the ecosystems in which they lived. One of these films, bringing to life ideas improvised with the participant, featured a young man, James, shown entering an old-style phone booth to make a call near his home in a northern regional town. The enacted call involves James having a conversation with future self and asking questions about his own future and that of his town and the world in general. Each scene of the film shows him becoming older as his surroundings change, until he is pretending to be his future self, aged 60. The film is intercut with documentary-style footage, showing James at his current age walking in his neighbourhood and scenes from the built and natural environments of his region demonstrating the drastic changes it has undergone. Sjöberg suggests that through films such as these, participants can co-create documented scenes from their imagined futures that render them situated and material, making explicit connections between the past and present experiences and their imagined futures.

A hauntological approach has also been proposed by anthropologists seeking to incorporate critical perspectives into ethnographic scholarship. Building on hauntological theory and Derrida's initial stance that making ghosts visible is a move towards social justice (Chapter 1), some anthropologists argue that all of us are in some way or another haunted by the past. Engaging with this idea, Sadeq Rahimi (2021) speculates about how to anthropologically investigate the hauntology of everyday life as a method for understanding power relations. As Byron Good, Andrea Chiovenda and Sadeq Rahimi (Good et al., 2022) have observed, people in contemporary societies are constantly haunted by historical inequities, violence, forced displacement, exploitation, racialism, colonialism, humans' abuse of the natural world and reactionary efforts to silence the past. These hauntings often inspire anxieties about futures, captured in Derrida's concept of the revenant (Chapter 1), involving seething affects that cannot easily be resolved, as it seems that the past is never settled despite the best efforts of powerful groups to repress it. Only by bringing these repressed secrets/ghosts into the light can past traumas be mourned. This ethical approach goes beyond fieldwork that identifies how ghosts and hauntings are understood in specific cultural contexts by turning attention to the positionality of anthropologists themselves: how to live with ghosts more justly, as Good and colleagues (paraphrasing Derrida) put it (Good et al., 2022).

Hauntology has been brought together with concepts of 'dark tourism' and climate change activism to address the cultural dimensions of the commemoration of disappearing glaciers (Varnajot & Salim, 2025). Dark tourism involves travellers visiting locations that are associated with loss, devastation, trauma, death or violence so as to engage in acts of witnessing or experiencing these affects. As such, these sites are redolent with powerful hauntological affective atmospheres (Chapter 1), which are major attracting forces for visitors. These practices have typically been associated with memorialising human suffering, but non-human entities have increasingly been incorporated into dark tourism. Melting glaciers have become a key symbol of the climate emergency, considered as geographical spectres, which are neither invisible nor visible, dead nor alive. In some places, funerals for vanished glaciers have been organised by local people as a ritual of grief for the loss of what are significant geological entities in many cultures. Visiting locations, or 'traumascapes' (Varnajot & Salim, 2025) where glaciers have disappeared or are in the process of melting due to climate change can be a way of engaging through embodied senses with environmental devastation, mourning the losses and damage to ecosystems that have resulted. It can also lead to acts involving the 'arts of noticing' (as outlined by Tsing) that can potentially inspire people to take action to counter further environmental devastation.

An analysis of 'haunted life' in postcolonial Iraq following the 2023 US-led invasion involved ethnographic interviews with citizens to investigate how they imagine their futures (Andersen, 2025). The invasion led to promises made to achieve a 'new' Iraqi state based on democratic governance grounded in human rights and dignity. However, many of these promises were not met. Instead, in the intervening time, a state of impunity has been established in Iraq, involving extended periods of conflict and civil war. Iraqi citizens, some of whom have been subjected to torture and other forms of violence or have witnessed family members being taken by the regime ('disappeared'), must live with the deep insecurities fostered by the traumatic legacies of colonial and state-imposed violence, with little hope of restoration of justice. Some bear the embodied 'tattoos' of violence – scars, injuries, disabilities, chronic pain or missing teeth. Iraqis are left to make sense of their lives amidst the uncertainties, trauma and dread generated by legacies of violence and fear of its potential return.

REFERENCES

Andersen, H. (2025). Haunted life: Sovereignty, affect, and impunity in Iraq. *Middle East Critique*. https://doi.org/10.1080/19436149.2025.2556068

Appadurai, A. (2013). *The future as cultural fact: Essays on the global condition*. Verso.

Bourgeois, R., Karuri-Sebina, G., & Feukeu, K. E. (2024). The future as a public good: Decolonising the future through anticipatory participatory action research. *Foresight*, *26*(4), 533–549.

Boyer, P. (2020). Why divination? Evolved psychology and strategic interaction in the production of truth. *Current Anthropology*, *61*(1), 100–123.

Bryant, R., & Knight, D. M. (2019). *The anthropology of the future*. Cambridge University Press.

Comaroff, J., & Comaroff, J. L. (1999). Occult economies and the violence of abstraction: Notes from the South African postcolony. *American Ethnologist*, *26*(2), 279–303.

Cortez, A., McKoy, A., & Lizárraga, J. R. (2022). The future of young Blacktivism: Aesthetics and practices of speculative activism in video game play. *Journal of Futures Studies*, *26*(3), 53–70.

D'Angelo, L. (2015). 'Diamond mining is a chain'. Luck, blessing, and gambling in Sierra Leone's artisanal mines. *Critical African Studies*, *7*(3), 243–261.

EASA Future Anthropologies Network. (2017). Futures anthropologies manifesto. In J. F. Salazar, S. Pink, A. Irving, & J. Sjoberg (Eds.), *Anthropologies and futures: Researching emerging and uncertain worlds* (pp. 1–2). Bloomsbury Academic.

Elish, M. C., & boyd, d. (2018). Situating methods in the magic of Big Data and AI. *Communication Monographs*, *85*(1), 57–80.

Evans-Pritchard, E. E. (1937). *Witchcraft, oracles and magic among the Azande*. The Clarendon Press.

Gaibazzi, P., & Gardini, M. (2015). The work of fate and fortune in Africa. *Critical African Studies*, 7(3), 203–209.
Gell, A. (1992). *The anthropology of time: Cultural constructions of temporal maps and images*. Routledge.
Gell, A. (1998). Time and social anthropology. *Senri Ethnological Studies*, 45, 9–24.
Good, B. J., Chiovenda, A., & Rahimi, S. (2022). The anthropology of being haunted: On the emergence of an anthropological hauntology. *Annual Review of Anthropology*, 51, 437–453.
Gregory, K. (2019). Pushed and pulled to the internet: Self employment in the spiritual marketplace. *American Behavioral Scientist*, 63(2), 208–224.
Hanna, A., & Bender, E. M. (2024). Theoretical AI harms are a distraction: Fearmongering about artificial intelligence's potential to end humanity shrouds the real harm it already causes. *Scientific American*, 330(2). 10.1038/scientificamerican0224-69
Joronen, M., Tawil-Souri, H., Amir, M., & Griffiths, M. (2021). Palestinian Futures: Anticipation, imagination, embodiments. Introduction to special issue. *Geografiska Annaler: Series B, Human Geography*, 103(4), 277–282.
Kazubowski-Houston, M., & Auslander, M. (2021). Introduction: In search of lost futures. In M. Kazubowski-Houston & M. Auslander (Eds.), *In search of lost futures: Anthropological explorations in multimodality, deep interdisciplinarity, and autoethnography* (pp. 1–18). Springer International Publishing.
Kissman, K. (1990). The role of fortune telling as a supportive function among Icelandic women. *International Social Work*, 33(2), 137–144.
Kravel-Tovi, M., & Bilu, Y. (2008). The work of the present: Constructing messianic temporality in the wake of failed prophecy among Chabad Hasidim. *American Ethnologist*, 35(1), 64–80.
Malinowski, B. (1994). *Argonauts of the Western Pacific: An account of native enterprise and adventure in the archipelagoes of Melanesian New Guinea*. Routledge. (Original work published 1922).
Marín González, K. (2025). The future arrives every 45 days: Temporal imaginaries and the coca assemblage in Sierra de la Macarena, Colombia. *Revista Colombiana de Antropología*, 61(1). https://doi.org/10.22380/2539472x.2818
Mauss, M. (2005). *A general theory of magic*. Routledge. (Original work published 1950).

Moeran, B., & de Waal Malefyt, T. (2018). Magical capitalism: An introduction. In B. Moeran & T. de Waal Malefyt (Eds.), *Magical capitalism: Enchantment, spells, and occult practices in contemporary economies* (pp. 1–44). Springer International Publishing.

Munn, N. D. (1992). The cultural anthropology of time: A critical essay. *Annual Review of Anthropology*, *21*, 93–123.

Pink, S. (2025). Trusted emplaced futures. In J. Glückler, M. Garschagen, & R. Panitz (Eds.), *Placing the future* (pp. 185–198). Springer Nature Switzerland.

Pink, S., Pinyon, Z., Duque, M., & Lundberg, R. (2024). Cross-sectoral futures: Futures anthropology and epistemic companions. *Anthropology in Action*, *31*(3), 7–17.

Pink, S., & Salazar, J. F. (2020). Anthropologies and futures: Setting the agenda. In J. F. Salazar, S. Pink, A. Irving, & J. Sjoberg (Eds.), *Anthropologies and futures: Researching emerging and uncertain worlds* (pp. 3–22). Routledge.

Poelina, A., Perdrisat, M., Wooltorton, S., & Mulligan, E. L. (2023). Feeling and hearing Country as research method. *Environmental Education Research*, 29(10), 1486–1501.

Rahimi, S. (2021). *The hauntology of everyday life*. Springer.

Ringel, F. (2016). Beyond temporality: Notes on the anthropology of time from a shrinking fieldsite. *Anthropological Theory*, *16*(4), 390–412.

Salazar, J.F. (2017) Speculative fabulation: researching worlds to come in Antarctica. In J.F. Salazar, S. Pink, S., A. Irving., & J. Sjoberg (Eds.), *Anthropology and futures: Researching emerging and uncertain worlds* (pp. 151–170). Routledge.

Salazar, J. F., Pink, S., Irving, A., & Sjoberg, J. (2017). *Anthropologies and futures: Researching emerging and uncertain worlds*. Bloomsbury.

Sjöberg, J. (2020). Ethno science fiction: Projective improvisations of future scenarios and environmental threat in the everyday life of British youth. In J. F. Salazar, S. Pink, A. Irving, & J. Sjöberg (Eds.), *Anthropologies and futures* (pp. 171–188). Routledge.

Skovgaard-Smith, I., & Hirst, A. (2023). Marcel Mauss and the magical agents of our time. *Journal of Classical Sociology*, 24(2), 171–185.

Tedlock, B. (2001). Divination as a way of knowing: Embodiment, visualisation, narrative, and interpretation. *Folklore*, *112*(2), 189–197.

Tedlock, B. (2006). Toward a theory of divinatory practice. *Anthropology of Consciousness*, 17(2), 62–77.

Terry, N., Castro, A., Chibwe, B., Karuri-Sebina, G., Savu, C., & Pereira, L. (2024). Inviting a decolonial praxis for future imaginaries of nature: Introducing the entangled time tree. *Environmental Science & Policy*, *151*. https://doi.org/10.1016/j.envsci.2023.103615

Tsing, A. L. (2015). *The mushroom at the end of the world: On the possibility of life in capitalist ruins*. Princeton University Press.

van Voorst, R. (2024). Anthropological fiction: Why anthropologists should dare to weave speculation through academic narratives. *Etnofoor*, *36*(1), 13–30.

Varnajot, A., & Salim, E. (2025). The hauntology of climate change: Glacier retreat and dark tourism. *Tourism Geographies*, 27(1), 102–119.

Velasco-Herrejón, P., Bauwens, T., & Calisto Friant, M. (2022). Challenging dominant sustainability worldviews on the energy transition: Lessons from Indigenous communities in Mexico and a plea for pluriversal technologies. *World Development*, *150*. https://www.sciencedirect.com/science/article/pii/S0305750X21003405

Wallis, R. J. (2017). Witchcraft and magic in the age of anthropology. In O. Davies (Ed.), *The Oxford illustrated history of witchcraft and magic* (pp. 227–257). Oxford University Press.

Wooltorton, S., White, P., Palmer, M., & Collard, L. (2020). Learning cycles: Enriching ways of knowing place. *Australian Journal of Environmental Education*, 37(1). 1017/aee.2020.15

4

SOCIOLOGIES AND GEOGRAPHIES OF FUTURES

SOCIOLOGIES OF FUTURES

Sociologists have traditionally been somewhat reluctant to engage in futures studies. However, in recent publications, calls for a sociology of futures have begun and suggestions for methods to investigate everyday futures have been outlined. In 2023, British sociologists Susan Halford and Dale Southerton (2023) published an editorial for *Sociology* journal's special issue on the theme of 'Sociologies of the Future and the Future of Sociology'. Their editorial noted that despite an initial interest in futures in early sociological inquiry, in the twentieth century, there was a progressive withdrawal from studying this topic, as sociology became formalised as a discipline and sought to distinguish itself from other social sciences. The future was positioned as too unknowable and unpredictable to be amenable to formal sociological study. Dominant modes of empirical research became focused on identifying current social trends and experiences, and futures research became viewed as the domain of the arts and humanities.

In the 1960s and 1970s, sociologists in the USA were proclaiming the study of futures as an important topic for sociology – or indeed, as the future of sociology. For example, writing in 1971 in *The American Sociologist* journal, Bettina Huber and Wendell Bell (1971) sought to explore the sociological possibilities of the study of the future, referring to the 'new science' of 'futurology' or

DOI: 10.4324/9781003726579-4

'futuristics'. They envisaged a new interdisciplinary field of study that would cut across the social sciences in the united purpose to study science, values and policy issues related to the future and investigate struggles over controlling it, thereby contributing to how futures are made. For Huber and Bell, these investigations should include casting the spotlight on how sociology itself helps shape the future. They argue that '[t]he main purpose of the sociology of the future is to construct pictures of what the future of the world's various societies could – and should – be like based upon scientific study of all possibilities, probabilities, preferences, and policies' (Huber & Bell, 1971, p. 288). It is evident in these discussions that at least some sociologists wanted to contribute to this new scientistic approach to researching and predicting futures. At this time, it was argued that the distinctive approach that sociology could offer was in identifying the roles played by social indicators, structures and values in futures thinking, including better understanding of how members of the public envisage futures and what future-facing policies they would accept.

Reflecting 30 years later on his predictions on the sociology of the future, Wendell Bell (1999) noted that they had largely not come to fruition: sociologists had not enthusiastically embraced futurology as a topic of inquiry. Bell had observed the study of futures more generally had, for the large part, 'moved off campus', becoming an applied professional practice rather than an academic research topic. He also referred to the lack of coherence in futures studies at the time at which he was writing and criticised the lack of scientific rigour in the social research that was conducted by futurists, who often lacked sociological training. Bell further remarked that the open-door policy of futurist conferences meant that even what he viewed as 'totally nutty' and fraudulent ideas received serious attention (Bell, 1999, p. 297). However, Bell did give kudos to those futurists whom he considered to adopt a realist approach, as he was concerned about the subjective and political nature of direction in which he saw American sociology as heading. In this reflection, therefore, Bell (1999, pp. 301–302) was advancing an unapologetically conservative and positivist argument. He considered the best sociology to be 'pure science' that had no 'reformist purposes' or 'fanatical ideology' and was able to be 'value explicit' in supporting principles that he believed were important.

Some monographs using social and cultural theory to understand futures have been published since the early years of this century. These include *Future Matters* by Barbara Adam and Chris Groves (2007), building on Adam's influential theorising of the sociology of time. Two other notable sociological monographs by well-known sociologists also appeared (both published posthumously): *What is the Future?* by John Urry (2016) and Zygmund Bauman's *Retrotopia* (2017).

Urry's book (2016) explored how contemporary Western societies understand, articulate and imagine futures, with a focus on manufacturing, urban mobilities, energy and climate change. He identified three main approaches to anticipating futures in the social sciences at the time at which he was writing. The first approach is the individualistic model of human action that assumes rational responses to opportunities and risks: largely expounded in economics and psychology. This approach has been subject to criticism for its overly rationalistic perspective and lack of recognition of social ties and social roles. A second set of theories emphasises the role played by socioeconomic structures and institutions such as the family, educational settings and the workplace, adopting a classical sociological perspective that sees individuals as constrained or influenced by social roles. Urry observed that this approach has been criticised for denying people's agency and not accounting for the dynamism and unpredictability of social structures and institutions and the impacts of social conflict in changing visions of the future. The third approach identified by Urry was complexity theory, which he saw as beginning to be incorporated across the social sciences, including in sociology. Urry saw this approach as superior to the other two, as he thought it to be less reductive as well as incorporating understanding of both individual agency and social structures.

In his book, Bauman (2017) drew on his long-standing theory of liquid modernity and liquid societies. Bauman characterised liquid modernity as characterised by a focus on the individual over the collective, so that people are encouraged to think of themselves as autonomous agents making their own destinies and living for the present through consumption. In this context, people feel unmoored, demonstrating a longing for recuperating lost shared values and a sense of community institutions rather than thinking realistically and hopefully about the future. 'Retrotopia', as Bauman defined it, refers to what he saw as the growing tendency in Western societies to turn away from a belief in the utopian value of constructing a better future, wanting to return to a romanticised and often mythical idealised past. He contrasted these nostalgic visions with imaginaries of the future which portray it as largely dystopian. In advancing his theory of a better way of future thinking, Bauman was inspired by Pope Francis' words of hope in reorienting ideas of the future towards more utopian visions, building on the concept of using the capacity for dialogue between nations and social groups and the art of living together to create a common future for the globe. Essentially, therefore, Bauman was arguing for moving from individualism to community thinking and developing a truly public life in the interests of building a more just future for all.

Adam and Groves' *Future Matters* (2007) focuses on how futures are both imagined and made by people. Barbara Adam is a leading sociologist of time who has published extensively on the social dimensions of futures thinking. Her book with Chris Groves addresses the complex interactions between action, knowledge and ethics in futures thinking, asking to what extent people and social groups should take responsibility for crafting better futures. Adam and Groves use the word 'taming' to describe how societies want to manage futures in a context in which there is constant change, insecurity and uncertainty, and refer to 'competence in futurity' as a pursuit which is aspired to as part of an urge to make change. Future thinking, from Adam and Groves' perspective, is part of rationalist efforts to both work towards change and do so in a way that quells uncertainty as much as possible. They make the important point that historic modes of divination (Chapter 2) relied on accessing the future beyond the human senses. These practices assumed that the future had been pre-determined, and that humans needed methods to uncover these existing futures. The major difference in contemporary societies, Adam and Groves suggest, is that the future has now become commodified: for example, through futures trading for economic benefit, and as part of the insurance and strategic foresight industries, which are also mostly tied to commercial and quantifiable signals of social, environmental and economic changes. They describe these futures as superficial and empty, disembedded as they are from socio-spatial and embodied contexts in which futures are lived.

Since publishing this book, Adam has continued and further developed her scholarship on the sociology of futures. In two recent articles, she (Adam, 2023, 2024) drew attention to the continuing lack of recognising sociomaterialities in social science approaches towards engaging with what she calls 'the not yet' and 'futures in the making'. She points out that futures are continually made every day, across the full breadth of institutions, identities and social groups: from the individual and the family to the sites of politics, law and the economy. Further, the future can never be known with any certainty and knowledge about it must be based on past evidence. There are layers upon layers of past and present futures entangled with future presents and future pasts. People experience, conceptualise and enact these temporalities simultaneously as they move through their life course. Adam (2023, p. 280) sums up that 'engagement with the future is a confrontation with imperfect knowledge, ignorance, even non-knowledge'. It is therefore a problematic domain of inquiry for sociologists and other social researchers. She further (2024) points out that sociologists and other social theorists have struggled to deal with the long distant past as well as with time scales beyond the near future. Adam therefore calls for a renewed social theory of the future that can acknowledge these vast temporal scales and for critical engagement with complex and unpredictable futures in the making that brings together disparate forms of knowledges and perspectives in new ways.

SOCIOLOGIES OF EXPECTATIONS, ANTICIPATION, RISK AND UNCERTAINTY

The sociologies of expectations, anticipation, risk and uncertainty have each developed independently, with some crossovers. These subfields all have a futures orientation but different theoretical and methodological underpinnings.

Drawing predominantly on science and technology studies, the sociology of expectations recognises the openness of the future. Scholars in this field address the politics and dynamics of expectations and promises about ventures in science and technology, as well as the sociomaterialities of how they are enacted (Brown & Michael, 2003). Enactments of the future are positioned as performative in the present, enrolling participants who will go on to shape or anticipate such futures (Sahakian et al., 2023). These enactments play a role in developing relationships between social groups, with social actors seeking to legitimate the use of some resources over others to achieve their desired visions of the future. It is in this way that expectations and promises about the future are often political, as they involve struggles over who has the power to enact the futures they want and can access the cultural or economic resources to achieve this (Tutton, 2023).

The concept of sociotechnical imaginaries is also frequently used in science and technology studies to investigate future-oriented predictions about novel technologies or services in public forums or industry publications. Sociotechnical imaginaries are a specific type of social imaginary (Chapter 1). They have been described as collective and publicly circulated visions, operating as 'powerful cultural resources' and persuasive infrastructures for planning and making sense of new technologies (Jasanoff & Kim, 2013, p. 190). These imaginaries can be about future uses of novel technologies or relate to 'actually existing' technologies that have recently been introduced and about which publics are still learning (Sismondo, 2020). They enact promissory narratives of what new technologies can offer in such forums as news stories, government announcements, policy documents and corporate websites. As such, sociotechnical imaginaries are integral to performances and enactments of futures, serving an economic and political purpose in rhetorical attempts to persuade publics that these technologies are useful, safe and effective.

For sociologists of expectations, everyday practices play a vital role in contributing to futures imaginaries and experiences. They have shown that there can be major differences in the ways that futures are discussed in public forums and people's everyday experiences of and feelings about futures. In arguing this point, Michael (2017) makes a distinction between what he calls 'Big Futures' compared with 'Little Futures'. Big Futures, in Michael's conceptualisation, refer to sociotechnical imaginaries about novel technological developments that are positioned as widespread, far-reaching and large-scale. These imaginaries are typically generated by actors with vested interests in promoting these technologies. By contrast, Little Futures, as the term suggests, are smaller-scale, more mundane and less revolutionary. Little Futures are the imaginaries enacted and sited in everyday contexts for publics and stakeholders who are attempting to make sense of what the implications are for their lives. As Michael argues, Big Futures imaginaries are directed at enrolling actors in the cause of enacting the practices that are required to achieve futures imaginaries. However, Big Futures are not necessarily accepted by publics. They are often contested, and publics are called upon to make sense of how best to respond. Little Futures can generate new directions for Big Futures, just as Big Futures can circumscribe how Little Futures are imagined and enacted.

These perspectives provide important insights into the Big and Little imaginaries and activities related to emerging technologies. For example, Jeroen Oomen and colleagues (2022) explored the question of how imagined futures become socially performative. Adopting a practice-based and dramaturgical approach, they suggest focusing on the act of futuring: that is, 'the identification, creation and dissemination of images of the future shaping the possibility space for action, thus enacting relationships between past, present and future' (Oomen et al., 2022, p. 253). A practice approach to futuring investigates how sociotechnical imaginaries take material shape, bringing the future into the present. This includes analysis of narratives, imaginaries and discourses about the future in industry, government or popular cultural texts, or in sites such as museums, conventions, conferences or government agencies, and how they operate to persuade people to accept these visions so that they become collective imaginaries.

The sociology of anticipation, according to Iddo Tavory and Nina Eliasoph (2013), builds on the social theory of Pierre Bourdieu and Alfred Schutz, bringing together phenomenology and symbolic interaction theory with Weberian rational action theory. This approach positions people as engaging together in future thinking through social interactions but within social structures, identities and cultural notions of temporalities ('temporal landscapes'). It therefore sees future thinking as a collective phenomenon, in which people work together to organise and coordinate their futures. Tavory and Eliasoph use the term 'protentions' to encapsulate individuals' 'feel' for the immediate future, and 'trajectories', to refer to people's longer-term plans or aspirations. Both protentions and trajectories are socialised in specific cultural contexts, becoming practices and habits over time, but are also open to change as people interact with others through their lives.

The sociology of risk and uncertainty acknowledges that risks are future-oriented phenomena (Lupton, 2023). Assessments of risk involve making predictions about what hazards might affect people into the future. From a sociological dimension, researchers have explored lay risk practices and understandings, acknowledging that such activities and rationales are regular parts of everyday life. This scholarship identifies the mentalities that contribute to lay risk thinking in the context of the sociocultural and political contexts in which people live. A key issue highlighted in the sociology of risk and uncertainty is the emotional dimensions of risk thinking. Risk can never be separated from the affective dimensions of everyday life: particularly as anticipation of risk and actual risk-taking can be experienced across a range of emotions, including fear and anxiety but also excitement, joy and pleasure.

Bringing together the sociology of risk with that of anticipation, Giovanni Gasparini (2004) highlights the ways that anticipation often occurs in the interstices of everyday life, such as times of waiting or travelling between two destinations, and in what he calls 'marginal phenomena', or exceptions to the rule, such as moments of gift exchange, surprise, unexpected event, play or loss.

These moments are part of everyday life but distinct from its usual routines and expectations. For Gasparini, these moments may operate to help people prepare themselves for other unexpected events but can also intensify feelings of uncertainty, risk and insecurity. He gives the example of the 9/11 bombings in New York City, for which residents of that city were completely unprepared. This catastrophe drastically altered their concepts of security and led to changes in anticipating, preparing for and preventing future such events. For example, in the case of 9/11, long-term changes were made to airport security systems.

FEMINIST AND QUEER FUTURISMS

Feminist and queer futurisms have strong links to currents in social and cultural theory that have developed critical futures studies approaches. Feminist futurisms as a field of research has developed in tandem with feminist scholarship more broadly. Feminist theory challenges the normative Western concept of clock time and how it is used to discipline bodies and marginalise those (such as women, disabled people, racialised people) who are not considered to be 'properly' aligned to clock time and therefore as less productive for the capitalist economic system. According to Milojević (2008, p. 333), hegemonic time 'is western, Christian, linear, abstract, clock dominated, work oriented, coercive, capitalist, masculine and anti-natural'. To counter hegemonic time in futures thinking, Milojević argues for a relational and social constructionist concept of temporality, focusing on the gendered experience of time.

In a special issue on the topic published in the key journal *Futures* in 2008, the editors Ivana Milojević, Karen Hurley and Anne Jenkins noted that the last special issue in that journal that had focused on gender had been published 18 years ago (Milojević et al., 2008). They remark that since this time, little had changed in relation to the sociopolitical conditions faced globally: rapid social, economic and political change, crises, continuing problems that seemed resistant to futures thinking initiatives. Nor was there much evidence that approaches to futures thinking that were advocated in the 1989 special issue – adopting feminist theories and methods or reaching beyond masculinist, positivist and quantitative techniques – gained much traction in mainstream futures research.

In more recent scholarship, feminist materialism philosophy (Chapter 1) has shaped ideas of temporalities and futures. Barad's concept of spacetimemattering and other engagements with quantum theory have contributed to radical new ways of understanding futures. In her work, Felicity Colman (2023) develops a theory of 'quantum feminicity' as a way to bring feminist theory together with quantum ideas of time. She suggests that this approach serves to reconfigure systems of temporal order, thereby opening up new ways of thinking about futures. Both quantum and feminist materialism theory share the idea that reality is not fixed but is open to different possibilities, as different matter and agents become entangled and disentangled, opening up capacities for action and transformation. Quantum theory contributes concepts of the relativity of time and challenges the notion of causality. The absolutist Western and androcentric model of temporality and teleological narratives of progress that have been harnessed to capitalist economic systems are challenged by this perspective. For Colman, adopting a quantum feminicity approach moves critique beyond the individual to the collective (communities of humans and nonhuman agents) in acknowledging the interdependency of all things. This is the idea of spacetimemattering espoused by Barad when they were demonstrating how quantum theory can be used in feminist and other social theory to ask what can be different and conceptualise how things can be otherwise.

Nikki Fairchild (2023) similarly draws on theorists such as Karen Barad and Donna Haraway as well as Indigenous cosmologies to open possibilities for reimagining the nature of multiple futures. Fairchild develops the concept of feminist materialist relational time to highlight how the past/present/future are always already in the making and formed of intra-acting bodies with space and time. She provides an example from her own empirical research with early childhood student teachers visiting English historical sites of ancient woodland as part of thinking through the materiality and historicity of place–space. This embodied experience helped the student teachers to rethink hegemonic worldviews of place and space and become open to affirmative futures they could explore with the young children they would be teaching.

Queer futurisms scholarship engages with queer, feminist, Indigenous and other more-than-human theory in developing an approach to futures that goes beyond heteronormative, patriarchal and gendered assumptions about temporalities. As argued in Chapter 1, queering as a theoretical project can lead to transformative possibilities for these communities in which concrete utopian futures can be developed via the queer political imagination (Muñoz, 2009). These ideas can involve developing kinship and convivial flourishing for humans and all other species to challenge the competitive ethos promoted by dominant modes of future thinking. Queer scholars have emphasised that narratives of survival play a central role in processes of futures thinking for queer people and other marginalised communities whose lives are precarious and under threat. Rather than 'survival of the fittest', this counter-futurist ethos develops futures visions in which 'survival of the queerist' is the main objective (Cheilan, 2026). Contributors to queer futurisms scholarship have demonstrated the transformative and performative ways that futures can be queered through methods such as experimental autoethnography.

One example is Lisa Bradley's 'Life without Clocks' project (Bradley, 2026), in which she experimented with living for nearly two weeks without consulting any kind of clock to investigate how well her embodied and sensory perceptions of the world would challenge the norms of hegemonic time.

GEOGRAPHIES OF THE FUTURE

A distinctive paradigm of any type of geographic research is its focus on spatiality, including studying geological and climatic features and the other creatures that dwell with humans in ecosystems, as well as human-made features of landscapes and environments. Geographies of the future devote considerable attention to the relationships between the socio-spatialities and temporalities of futures, incorporating experiences and ideas of time, place and space into futures thinking.

Human geographer Ben Anderson (2010) has made major contributions to the cultural analysis of anticipation in the context of risk. He argued that the problematisation of the future, positioning it as a surprise, indeterminant or a disruption, has led to a proliferation of modes of anticipatory action in response. For Anderson, these actions have confronted geography with the topic of 'the future', raising questions about what futures are anticipated and how, how are they rendered actionable and what political and ethical consequences arise from acting in the present as an intervention into anticipated futures. He observes that statements about the future serve to configure it in certain defined ways which limit how the future can be acted upon. Anderson focuses on catastrophic risk, and how the anticipatory actions of pre-emption, precaution and preparedness have been deployed to govern such risk – and indeed, to configure the presence of the future in the current moment. He argues that through anticipatory practices and discourses of calculation, imagination (for example, qualitative forecasting and scenarios) and performances (such as war games and crisis simulations), any specific future is suspended between the here-and-now and an 'elsewhen or elsewhere ... made present while remaining absent' (Anderson, 2010, p. 783).

A recent overview of geographies of the future scholarship (Müller-Mahn et al., 2025) observes that for geographical inquiry that relies on scientific quantitative methods such as modelling, identification of trends and probability assessments, and which typically focus on topics such as environmental devastation, the future is now usually framed as a crisis rather than in optimistic ways. Such predictions tend to assume that little can be done in the present day to change the future. In contrast, these authors propose alternative approaches that offer 'political and poetic' ways to imagine geographies of hope and survival, aiming to intervene to change the future rather than simply accept its inevitability. It is evident that at least some researchers in geography are interested in developing scholarship that is overtly activist in intention, by exploring how publics can engage in prefigurative politics ('being the change you want to see') or counter-futures related to current crises such as climate change. Prefigurative politics involves social movements and collective action (for example, the feminist movement and Occupy Movement) that seek prefigurative action as a way to achieve change, thus combining creation with resistance. Such actions includes establishing schools, community healthcare facilities, festivals, food distribution centres, alternative economies or media centres that acted as models for the type of social organisation to which the activists aspire (Jeffrey & Dyson, 2020).

Geographers are also interested in the more-than-human dimensions of people's experiences of and imaginaries about futures. The concept of 'thick time' has been used in geographies of the future in ways that bring these issues to the fore. This concept was first used by South African artist William Kentridge (Blazwick & Breitwieser, 2016) to describe his creative work, in which he connects the times of past, present and future to a 'black hole': the space where everything disappears. For Kentridge, thick time is a practice by which the temporal crises accumulated over generations, coming into being through technologies of Western linear time and clock time, timekeeping, time-management and their resultant time-burdens, are confronted. Engaging in thick time practices involves slowing down and developing a resistant postcolonial and subjective experience of time, refusing Western normative framings. In Kentridge's multimedia work and installations, time is represented as overlaid with palimpsests of past times but also in a continuous looping, so that there is no apparent ending to time (see Chapter 2 for further discussion of palimpsestic time).

Thick time in the context of everyday crises has been developed in the work of researchers such as Ayona Datta (2022) to explore experiments with feminist urban futures in Delhi in the context of the COVID-19 pandemic. Datta argues that the early phase of COVID was a slow emergency which thickened intergenerational injustices and disrupted concepts of time. Time was both speeded up, as people came to terms with the rapid spread of the novel coronavirus, but also seemed suspended or slowed down as biopolitical mitigations such as institutional closures, curfews and lockdowns came into force. Datta used podcasts as a method for recording the experiences of young women's living in poverty in resettlement colonies in Delhi's urban peripheries. She captured these women's thick descriptions of time in the context of their domestic spaces, including how they imagined the future once the pandemic emergency had passed. Datta argues that thick time connects the biopolitical and clock time imposed by the state upon these women with the intimate domestic time of gendered struggles.

Other geographies of time have focused on how people incorporate references to space and spatiality into their futures thinking. They note that spatial metaphors and other features of language can be powerful in representing futures imaginaries: especially so when combined with existing material attributes to place and space that help to make futures seem more concrete and achievable (Müller-Mahn et al., 2025). One example of this type of scholarship is an analysis of the use of metaphor in the structure of futuristic buildings (some already built, others still on the drawing board), deconstructing the future-related messages the architects of these buildings were attempting to convey (Heinonen & Minkkinen, 2016). The study identified three categories in the vernacular of the buildings' design – nature metaphors, technological metaphors and social metaphors – and discussed how these metaphors convey meanings concerning how the future is envisaged. For example, some buildings engaging with nature/organic metaphors in their structure suggest a yearning for a future that returns to the simpler life of the distant past, while others, drawing on ecological thinking, suggest the possibility of alternative futures.

Some cultural geographers thinking about the future have engaged with speculative theory and methods in considering the embodied, sensory and more-than-human dimensions of imagining, performing and enacting futures. Indeed, scholars contributing to a subfield of geography entitled 'speculative geographies' have outlined such a project, defining speculation as involving the configuration of diverse plural narratives, recognition of multiple forms of knowledge and the development of interventions into possible futures that problematise present-day conditions (Williams & Keating, 2022). One such project investigated how the futures of nuclear waste have been articulated in archival, aesthetic and speculative sources. The researchers argued that drawing on past representations of nuclear waste – addressing the communication of 'nuclear memory' – provides a way for geographers to formulate alternative possibilities, helping them transfer knowledge and information about these materials into the future. This requires engaging with affective and non-representational modes of expression and the ways that both memories and futures imaginaries are embodied and tangible in place and space. It also involves recognising deep timescales while maintaining attention to the material politics of the here and now and how current actions will affect planetary futures (Keating & Storm, 2023).

Another project used collaging as a way of futures worldbuilding. Participants were invited to respond to the collages to imagine how relationships with social robots would take place in near-future public settings (Sumartojo et al., 2021). Rather than deploying this method to generate certainties about futures, these researchers chose to work with uncertainty, characterising it as generative for more open-ended futures thinking. They therefore developed visual materials that were explicitly ambiguous, seeking to invite their research participants to reflect on the past and the present as part of their speculations about novel technologies. Photographs of public spaces that had been digitally manipulated by the researchers so that they were indeterminate locations were used as the settings for the collages, with robot images taken from publicly available images and human figures placed within the setting. Research participants were shown the collages in an online interview and asked about what they thought the purpose of the robots was and whether these technologies 'felt right' in those settings.

DYSTOPIAN FUTURES AND FUTURELESSNESS

Social researchers emphasise that futures thinking undertaken at the social structural and institutional level is always political, associated with vested interests and desire for power. The future can also be viewed as itself a political problem. Sociologists and geographers of futures have identified the seemingly intractable pessimism that pervades future-oriented imaginaries, noting that in the wealthy countries of the Global North, the future is increasingly imagined as disastrous, with little hope for redemption. The world seems to be stuck in a permacrisis, with many people feeling as if they have no future due to the difficult circumstances in which they are living.

Sociologist Richard Tutton (2023) believes that modern European societies are characterised by a pervading feeling of futurelessness developing since World War II, particularly among young people, as they see little action on climate change, improvements in standards of living or better job provision from governments. He outlines an agenda for the study of futurelessness which involves better understanding of which social groups and subgroups feel this way about their futures, to what extent it is part of their everyday lives and the relationship between socioeconomic disadvantage, ethnicity/cultural heritage, age and feelings of futurelessness. Cultural geographer Kezia Barker (2025) has pondered why people seem to be 'sleepwalking' in response to the climate change emergency, denying the risks that humans and planet face and demonstrating apathy about making change happen to alleviate these risks. One explanation for this 'unfeeling' response advanced by Barker is that people in Western societies have become alienated and detached from the natural world to such an extent that they are unable to make the connection between their lives and that of the ecosystems of which they are part (and to which they are causing damage).

Social theorists have also expressed a loss of hope and growing despair about the worsening state of global politics and environmental devastation. The late Bruno Latour was well-known for his scholarship in the philosophy of science and technology. His work gradually became more pessimistic as he observed the lack of action in his lifetime on environmental devastation and climate change. In his final book, *After Lockdown: A Metamorphosis*, and written in the first year of the COVID pandemic, Latour (2021) ruminated on whether humans would realise the lessons of COVID: particularly in relation to the continuing devastation wrought by humans on the natural world. Latour had long written about environmental crises, noting how little action had occurred despite years of science and activism. Anticipating a possible global collapse due to climate change, he viewed the restrictions on movement introduced by governments to attempt to contain the spread of the COVID virus as merely a forerunner of what was to come if privileged people living in the Global North did not radically change their behaviours.

The interdisciplinary field of extinction studies offers perhaps the bleakest futures thinking across the humanities and social sciences (O'Key, 2023; Symons & Garlick, 2020). In this literature, extinction refers to the Sixth Mass Extinction event, or the crisis currently facing the planet due to human-caused environmental devastation, habitat loss and the resultant loss of species and decline in biodiversity. This extinction event, unlike the previous ones faced by the earth's ecosystems across its deep history, is therefore conceptualised as a socioecological phenomenon, in which the natural temporalities of climate change and extinction have been disrupted. Such critiques call attention to the intersections of the capitalist ethos of extraction, together with the forces of globalisation, industrialisation, imperialism and colonialism, in contributing to this ecological devastation. These analyses are situated within specific ecosocial and geographical contexts to draw out the complexities of how and why extinction is taking place and what the future may hold for biodiversity.

The term 'living in the ruins' is sometimes used to articulate how humans experience, bear witness to and imagine the realities of ecocide processes which have no bounded temporal limits while humans continue to heedlessly inflict violence on other species (Symons & Garlick, 2020). Collective nostalgia for an imagined past often plays a role in people's efforts to protect threatened species and to speculate about a future in which these species continue to thrive rather than being lost. Holding on to hope is a way that people manage their feelings such as grief and anger about ecocide while simultaneously believing that change can happen, even as there is little evidence that humans are doing anything meaningful to prevent this for future generations. In this way, human responses to the extinction crisis combine history, absence, nostalgia, hauntology and memory with futures thinking (Symons & Garlick, 2020; Wrigley, 2020).

SOCIOLOGIES OF LAY FUTURING PRACTICES

Chapter 2 provided an overview of lay futuring beliefs and practices in human history since antiquity and highlighted their entanglements with religious, spiritual, magical and scientific belief systems. Social research shows that in contemporary times, magical, spiritual and religious beliefs continue to underpin futures thinking, even among people who might otherwise see themselves as scientific and rational.

Astrology has been a major mode of futures thinking for millennia across the globe (Chapter 2). It remains very popular in the current day and is a hugely profitable industry. Horoscopes are regularly published in news sites and magazines; there are a plethora of books about astrology, professional astrologers offering online services and apps and social media posts as well. Contributing to its popularity in the West is the intersections between magical capitalism (Chapter 3), new age spiritualism and pseudo-scientific and pop psychology discourses concerning personality, self-improvement, self-understanding and identity. Nearly everyone knows what their 'star/zodiac' sign is and what it suggests about their personality (Noy et al., 2025). Surveys of undergraduates majoring in science at a US university over a 20-year period showed that a large majority considered astrology to be 'very' or 'sort of' scientific (Sugarman et al., 2011). However, other US-based research demonstrates that most Americans disagree that astrology can be used to accurately predict their future. Instead, they see astrology, and particularly zodiac signs, as useful for giving them insights about their personality or behaviour (Noy et al., 2025). A Pew Research Center survey conducted in 2024 found that 30% of Americans consult astrology or a horoscope, tarot cards or fortune tellers at least once a year, but most engage in these practices for fun rather than using them to make major decisions or believing in predictions about their destinies. Younger adults, especially younger women, were more likely to believe in astrology and consult horoscopes, as were people who identified as lesbian, gay, bisexual or transgender, Black people, and those with lower education and income levels (Rotolo, 2025).

Investigations into how professionals deal with risk have revealed that even in this context, rituals similar to traditional forms of divination (Chapter 2) often come into play. For example, a qualitative study of Canadian entrepreneurs (Ganzin et al., 2019) found that they often drew on magical thinking when attempting to mitigate the risks concerning an uncertain future. The study identified a cluster of beliefs used by these entrepreneurs to maintain their energy and focus. They adhered to a quasi-religious cosmological system that privileged elements such as 'finding one's path', 'obtaining the answers' and 'being at peace'. In another example, a Taiwanese study using a survey to identify patterns of engagement in fortune telling surprisingly found that city dwellers, those who were highly educated and those with better levels of scientific knowledge were more likely to participate in these practices (Shein et al., 2014).

Further insights were provided by Timothy Neale's (2023) ethnographic observations of the operations of a bushfire control centre in southeast Australia during a period of high fire risk. Neale noticed that in the pursuit of the control over uncertainty promised in the very name of this 'control centre', divining rituals played a key role. Fire analysts use a range of information sources and prediction techniques each day to attempt to anticipate where fires might break out in the region, including reviewing weather forecasts, assessments about vegetation moisture levels and data about potential power-line failures or lightning strikes that might ignite a fire. There are very high levels of uncertainty in these predictions, often involving intuition and guesswork ('gut feeling') rather than accurate scientific assessment, such that colleagues refer to these forecasting techniques as 'voodoo' or 'black magic'. Nonetheless, these acts of divination bear significant social and symbolic weight as a way of demonstrating that the control centre is doing what is expected of it. These contribute to processes of normalising and domesticating environmental crises, and showing 'something is being done' by governments without seriously confronting the broader problems that are causing such risks (such as climate change).

The relationship between people's beliefs about how much control they have over their destinies and their spiritual, religious or superstitious beliefs has been the focus of several studies globally. A Turkish study (Baruh et al., 2025) involved a survey investigating people's likelihood of engaging in future health prediction as a function of their fatalism, future time orientation, superstition and history of chronic disease. It found that people living with a chronic disease were more likely to have higher fatalism, which, in turn, decreased their likelihood of providing a rating for their future health. Further, more superstitious individuals were less likely to report expectations about future health. The authors suggest that some people may avoid sharing predictions about their future health because they fear it can invite negative outcomes by 'tempting fate'.

The concept of tempting fate itself rests on the idea that a person's actions or words can cause bad luck, 'jinxing' success or a positive outcome. In Anglophone literature, the expression has been traced back to the 1300s in relation to the need not to invite hubris by 'tempting God' through suggesting that human action can have precedence over divine providence (Risen & Gilovich, 2018). In contemporary societies, the phrase is frequently used to refer to choosing to engage in activities that are highly risky, ignoring culturally shared superstitions (for example, walking under a ladder, doing something important on an inauspicious date or purchasing a property with an unlucky number), making overly confident or presumptuous claims about future success, or being greedy or otherwise wanting too much from life and expecting good fortune repeatedly. There are strong moral associations with applying the phrase to the actions of oneself or others. The central suggestion is that people lack a degree of control and certainty in their destinies and that fate or misfortune can occur randomly. The phrase 'knock on wood', (accompanied with an actual knocking of the fist against a wooden surface if one is available) has a similar meaning. Actions such as crossing one's fingers (or simply intoning the phrase 'fingers crossed') are also considered to be practices inviting good fortune.

This notion of needing to avoid tempting fate is an intriguing concept in relation to futures thinking. It suggests that it is better to avoid making any sort of prediction about one's destiny, as the prediction itself invites the possibility of a poor outcome. There are other superstitious rituals across cultures in which people engage to ward off the jinx of tempting fate or otherwise attempt to stave off misfortune. For example, in Chinese culture, many words or expressions that are semantically neutral have become considered to be taboo or good luck because they are associated linguistically with factual taboo/good luck words or expressions. Chinese people use the term 'mouth luck' to describe the art of using language appropriately to invite good fortune or avoid bad luck (Yang, 2009). Several studies have demonstrated that professional athletes and sports fans often use charms, incantations or habits to promote the possibility of sporting success. A study of superstitious behaviour among American and Japanese professional baseball players found that such rituals include using a lucky toothbrush, using the same shower or eating the same type of food before each game, wearing certain articles of clothing, choosing the same spot to sit in the dugout and always using the same sporting equipment. For these elite sportsmen, engaging in these lucky practices was seen as a way of exerting control over the uncertainties that influence the outcome of the game (Burger & Lynn, 2005).

As explained in Chapter 2, divination practices have historically been exchanged across global cultures. This remains the case in contemporary times. Traditional techniques that were popular in one part of the world now have been taken up in other regions. The development of mass media, telephony, video recordings, home computing and digital technologies such as websites, social media platforms and apps has contributed to the globalisation of these practices.

A study of divination practices in contemporary Japan conducted in the mid-1990s identified practices that used direct communication (face-to-face) and in-direct channels (Kentarō, 1995). The classic and most popular diviners at that time were street fortune tellers, readily available for consultation in entertainment precincts with booths or tables made available for clients to engage with them. There were also home-based fortune tellers, who operated out of their own homes or in a private office, usually by appointment. By the 1980s, divination was offered by phone services, and by the 1990s, touring fortune tellers who travelled to special functions became available. Palmistry and physiognomy were the most common divination practices offered by street fortune tellers, followed by augury and Eastern astrology. Home-based fortune tellers included Western divination techniques, such as tarot card readings and Western astrology, among their services. Non-direct channels for fortune telling included regular columns by diviners in magazines based on Western astrology, annual almanacs based on Eastern astrology, books to help people practice fortune telling themselves, television programs and segments on the topic and computerised divination machines available in shopping centres or programs for home computers.

By the early 2010s, the Japanese divination boom had expanded into a range of diverse practices combining traditional Japanese culture with Western divination (Miller, 2011). One example is car *feng shui*, translating a Chinese traditional custom (Chapter 2) for Japanese female car owners. This practice involved the provision of advice for how to select auspicious tyre styles and accessories for the car. Bars and cafes in Tokyo were offering tarot card readings, and a range of other divinatory methods had sprung up to serve a growing clientele. Features of Japanese culture were incorporated into tarot card decks and computer games and apps, catering to themes or genres such as manga, anime and cute cuddly characters drawing on Japanese *kawaii* culture

China similarly experienced 'fortune-telling fever' in the 1980s, following the death of Mao Zedong in 1976. As part of the rise to power of the Chinese Communist Party following World WarI II, beliefs and practices such as religion, shamanism, fortune telling, witchcraft and geomancy that were characterised by the Party's leaders as 'feudal superstitions' were stamped out. They were deemed to be incompatible with modern ideals of science and rationality that were considered important in rebuilding the Chinese nation. Following Mao's death, however, and together with the social and economic reforms introduced by the new leader Deng Xiaoping, religious, spiritual and other mystical beliefs were again allowed. Fortune tellers and diviners became immensely popular, reviving ancient practices such as physiognomy and astrology. Practitioners were careful to position themselves as allies of the state by appealing to politically acceptable notions of the revitalisation of Chinese cultural nationalism and scientific advancement. They filled the cultural vacuum left by Maoist Marxist ideologies with a familiar belief system that offered spiritual meaning and enchantment together with control and purpose to clients, as well as aligning with the new spirit of commercialisation promoted by the Chinese Communist Party (Baum, 2021).

Practices that remain popular in China and among Chinese diaspora include communicating with ancestors or divinities through mediums, fate calculation techniques, calendar horoscopy, *feng shui* and palmistry, as well as Western traditional mantic arts such as esoteric tarot and Western-style astrology (Zongli, 2022). Young Chinese people in particular have taken up tarot, spurred on by videos of readings shared on social media which began to appear in China in the 2000s. Interest in the practice was later heightened by BiliBili, one of China's largest video-sharing platforms, when it began hosting interactive tarot-reading videos in 2019, presenting it as an exotic divination practice. Over time, the Chinese video makers of the tarot readings strategically aligned their discourses and practices with those of dominant cultural values, including the state's criticisms of superstition. This was achieved by contending that the readings were for entertainment purposes rather than true divination, and promoting the idea of the good Chinese citizen as someone who resolves their life difficulties while maintaining harmonious relationships with others (Fu et al., 2022).

With the advent of digital apps, social media platforms and generative AI services, lay divination practices around the world have been further digitised, offering new ways for corporations to profit from magical capitalism. The phenomenon of 'digital necromancy' has been identified, involving people's use of digital technologies to communicate with or create digital versions of dead loved ones. Examples include Facebook memorial sites where users write posts as if the deceased person is still alive, chatbots that pretend to speak to a digital version of someone who has died and applications allowing people to animate dead relatives' still images with short videos (Morse, 2024; Zohny, 2025). Axel Gruvæus (2023, p. 104) has described these technologies as creating 'functional ghosts' which can help extend people's digital presence beyond the grave for those in the present day. As such, digital necromancy is similar to the practices of spiritualism and seances that were popular in the early twentieth century (Chapter 2).

Other digital services offer people a way to have conversations with their own future selves using generative AI services (Pataranutaporn et al., 2024). TikTok memes and videos give people an avenue to express their hopes for a better world, while cyber spellbooks offer curses or spells to articulate frustrations and virtual reality (Kneese et al., 2025). Chatbots driven by algorithmic decision-making or large language models have been introduced as automated fortune tellers or spiritual guides for those wanting a conversation about their future. These technologies can imitate the listening and dialogic styles of human fortune tellers but are not necessarily trusted in the same way by those who seek such services. A study of how Chinese users engage with generative AI-based fortune telling, including ChatGPT and CeCe (a Chinese divination service) found that people who were looking for entertainment or psychological comfort were particularly receptive to the automated decision-making offered by these services. However, while the accessibility, convenience and efficiency offered by ChatGPT and CeCe were valued by users, these tools were viewed as lacking spiritual mystique. Those who had more significant decisions to make or questions to ask of these services were more cautious about accepting the results of their queries (Ling et al., 2026).

REFERENCES

Adam, B. (2023). Futures imperfect: A reflection on challenges. *Sociology*, 57(2), 279–287.

Adam, B. (2024). Tempering the not-yet: Towards a social theory for the Anthropocene. *European Journal of Social Theory*, 27(2), 191–208.

Adam, B., & Groves, C. (2007). *Future matters: Action, knowledge, ethics*. Brill.

Anderson, B. (2010). Preemption, precaution, preparedness: Anticipatory action and future geographies. *Progress in Human Geography*, 34(6), 777–798.

Barker, K. (2025). Anaesthetic worlds of denial: "sleepwalking" through climate catastrophe. In J. Johannes Glückler, M. Garschagen, & R. Panitz (Eds.), *Placing the future* (pp. 75–96). Springer.

Baruh, L., Sen, C. K. N., Cemalcilar, Z., & Kumkale, G. T. (2025). Let's not tempt fate: The influence of future time-orientation, fatalism, and superstition on willingness to report expectations about future health. *SAGE Open*, 15(1). https://doi.org/10.1177/21582440241300482

Baum, E. (2021). Enchantment in an age of reform: Fortune-telling fever in Post-Mao China, 1980s–1990s. *Past & Present*, 251(1), 229–261.

Bauman, Z. (2017). *Retrotopia*. Polity.

Bell, W. (1999). The sociology of the future and the future of sociology. *International Review of Sociology*, 9(3), 295–310.

Blazwick, I., & Breitwieser, S. (2016). *William Kentridge: Thick Time*. Whitechapel Art Gallery. https://books.google.com.au/books?id=RxDcDAEACAAJ

Bradley, L. (2026). Life without clocks: Experimental autoethnography for strange-ing time and queering futures, in and through higher education. *Futures*. https://www.sciencedirect.com/science/article/pii/S0016328725002010

Brown, N., & Michael, M. (2003). A sociology of expectations: Retrospecting prospects and prospecting retrospects. *Technology Analysis & Strategic Management*, *15*(1), 3–18.

Burger, J. M., & Lynn, A. L. (2005). Superstitious behavior among American and Japanese professional baseball players. *Basic and Applied Social Psychology*, *27*(1), 71–76.

Cheilan, L. (2026). Survival of the Queerest: Queer survival and future possibilities. *Futures*, *176*. https://www.sciencedirect.com/science/article/pii/S001632872600008X

Colman, F. (2023). Quantum feminicity: Modes of countermanding time. *Technophany. A Journal for Philosophy and Technology*, 2(1), 1–37.

Datta, A. (2022). 'Thick time': Experiments with feminist urban futures in community podcasts. *Geoforum*, *134*, 108–117.

Fairchild, N. (2023). Multiverse, feminist materialist relational time, and multiple future(s): (Re)configuring possibilities for qualitative inquiry. *Qualitative Inquiry*, *30*(6), 493–501.

Fu, H., Li, Y., & Lee, F. L. F. (2022). Techno-cultural domestication of online tarot reading in contemporary China. *Media, Culture & Society*, *45*(1), 74–91.

Ganzin, M., Islam, G., & Suddaby, R. (2019). Spirituality and entrepreneurship: The role of magical thinking in future-oriented sensemaking. *Organization Studies*, *41*(1), 77–102.

Gasparini, G. (2004). Anticipation and the surprises of everyday life. *Social Science Information*, 43(3), 339–348.

Gruvæus, A. (2023). Beyond peak death?-The advent of digital necromancy and functional ghosts. *Journal of Future Studies*, 27(3), 103–109.

Halford, S., & Southerton, D. (2023). What future for the sociology of futures? Visions, concepts and methods. *Sociology*, 57(2), 263–278.

Heinonen, S., & Minkkinen, M. (2016). Interpreting built cityscape: Deconstructing the metaphorical messages of futuristic buildings. *Futures*, *84*, 163–177.

Huber, B. J., & Bell, W. (1971). Sociology and the emergent study of the future. *The American Sociologist*, 6(4), 287–295.

Jasanoff, S., & Kim, S.-H. (2013). Sociotechnical imaginaries and national energy policies. *Science as Culture*, 22(2), 189–196.

Jeffrey, C., & Dyson, J. (2020). Geographies of the future: Prefigurative politics. *Progress in Human Geography*, 45(4), 641–658.

Keating, T. P., & Storm, A. (2023). Nuclear memory: Archival, aesthetic, speculative. *Progress in Environmental Geography*, 2(1–2), 97–117.

Kentarō, S. (1995). Divination in contemporary Japan: A general overview and an analysis of survey results. *Japanese Journal of Religious Studies*, 22(3/4), 249–266.

Kneese, T., Moro, J., & Vecchione, B. (2025). Algorithms and the occult, or chatbots are the new psychic friends network. *ASAP Review*. https://asapjournal.com/node/algorithms-and-the-occult-or-chatbots-are-the-new-psychic-friends-network/

Latour, B. (2021). *After lockdown: A metamorphosis*. Polity Press.

Ling, L., Zheng, X., Cao, G., & Ray, L. (2026). "Re-tell the fortune so I can believe it"*: How Chinese user communities engage with and interpret GenAI-based fortune telling*. ACM SIGCHI Conference on Computer Supported Cooperative Work & Social Computing (CSCW '26). https://arxiv.org/abs/2603.27784

Lupton, D. (2023). *Risk* (3rd ed.). Routledge.

Michael, M. (2017). Enacting Big Futures, Little Futures: Toward an ecology of futures. *The Sociological Review*, 65(3), 509–524.

Miller, L. (2011). Tantalizing tarot and cute cartomancy in Japan. *Japanese Studies*, 31(1), 73–91.

Milojević, I. (2008). Timing feminism, feminising time. *Futures*, 40(4), 329–345.

Milojević, I., Hurley, K., & Jenkins, A. (2008). Futures of feminism. *Futures*, 40(4), 313–318.

Morse, T. (2024). Digital necromancy: users' perceptions of digital afterlife and posthumous communication technologies. *Information, Communication & Society*, 27(2), 240–256.

Müller-Mahn, D., Runkel, S., Schlottmann, A., & Stephan, C. (2025). Geographies of the future. *Geographica Helvetica*, 80(3), 177–185.

Muñoz, J. E. (2009). *Cruising utopia: The then and there of queer futurity*. New York University Press.

Neale, T. (2023). Performing control. *American Ethnologist*, *50*(4), 568–581.

Noy, S., Siefke, A., Corcoran, K. E., & Scheitle, C. P. (2025). Contemporary views and uses of astrology in the United States: A descriptive, mixed-methods analysis. *Social Currents*, *12*(5), 456–471.

O'Key, D. (2023). Extinction in public: Thinking through the Sixth Mass Extinction, environmental humanities, and extinction studies. *Environmental Humanities*, *15*(1), 168–186.

Oomen, J., Hoffman, J., & Hajer, M. A. (2022). Techniques of futuring: On how imagined futures become socially performative. *European Journal of Social Theory*, *25*(2), 252–270.

Pataranutaporn, P., Winson, K., Yin, P., Lapapirojn, A., Ouppaphan, P., Lertsutthiwong, M., Maes, P., & Hershfield, H. E. (2024). Future you: a conversation with an AI-generated future self reduces anxiety, negative emotions, and increases future self-continuity. 2024 IEEE Frontiers in Education Conference (FIE), Washington.

Risen, J. L., & Gilovich, T. (2018). Understanding people's fear of tempting fate. *Journal of the Association for Consumer Research*, *3*(4), 599–611.

Rotolo, C. (2025). 30% of Americans consult astrology, tarot cards or fortune tellers. Pew Research Center. https://www.pewresearch.org/religion/2025/05/21/3-in-10-americans-consult-astrology-tarot-cards-or-fortune-tellers/

Sahakian, M., Moynat, O., Senn, W., & Moreau, V. (2023). How social practices inform the future as method: Describing personas in an energy transition while engaging with teleoaffectivities. *Futures*, *148*. https://www.sciencedirect.com/science/article/pii/S001632872300037X

Shein, P. P., Li, Y.-Y., & Huang, T.-C. (2014). Relationship between scientific knowledge and fortune-telling. *Public Understanding of Science*, *23*(7), 780–796.

Sismondo, S. (2020). Sociotechnical imaginaries: An accidental themed issue. *Social Studies of Science*, *50*(4), 505–507.

Sugarman, H., Impey, C., Buxner, S., & Antonellis, J. (2011). Astrology beliefs among undergraduate students. *Astronomy Education Review*, *10*(1). 10.3847/AER2010040

Sumartojo, S., Lundberg, R., Tian, L., Carreno-Medrano, P., Kulić, D., & Mintrom, M. (2021). Imagining public space robots of the near-future. *Geoforum*, *124*, 99–109.

Symons, K., & Garlick, B. (2020). Introduction: Tracing geographies of extinction. *Environmental Humanities*, *12*(1), 288–295.

Tavory, I., & Eliasoph, N. (2013). Coordinating futures: Toward a theory of anticipation. *American Journal of Sociology*, *118*(4), 908–942.

Tutton, R. (2023). The sociology of futurelessness. *Sociology*, *57*(2), 438–453.

Urry, J. (2016). *What is the future?* Polity.

Williams, N., & Keating, T. (2022). From abstract thinking to thinking abstractions: Introducing speculative geographies. In N. Williams & T. Keating (Eds.), *Speculative geographies: Ethics, technologies, aesthetics* (pp. 1–32). Springer Nature Singapore.

Wrigley, C. (2020). Nine lives down: Love, loss, and longing in Scottish wildcat conservation. *Environmental Humanities*, *12*(1), 346–369.

Yang, S. (2009). Purely linguistic taboo/good luck language and its impact on behaviors in China. *RASK: International Journal of Language and Communication*, *83*, 83–110.

Zohny, H. (2025). The specter of corporate necromancy: Who controls the dead in the age of digital doppelgängers? *The American Journal of Bioethics*, *25*(2), 113–115.

Zongli, L. (2022). Handbook of divination and prognostication in China. Part one: Introduction to the field. *Chinese Literature, Essays, Articles, Reviews*, 44, 301–307.

5

CREATIVE FUTURING

CREATIVE WRITING AND SPECULATIVE NARRATIVE APPROACHES

There are a plethora of literary and genre fiction and other forms of popular culture (television series, films, video games, graphic fiction) that imagine future worlds. The popularity of the genre of speculative fiction attests to the compelling and engaging nature of such narratives. Whether it is a video game such as *The Last of Us* (also adapted by Netflix as a television series) or classic science fiction by novelists such as Mary Shelley, Jules Verne, Ursula Le Guin, Octavia Butler, William Gibson or Margaret Atwood, speculative fiction offers a way for those who consume it to enter new future worlds. Speculative fiction narratives can also serve as a form of activism, awareness raising and resistance to contemporary social structures and inequalities, as well as challenging human practices that are causing environmental devastation.

Speculative narrative has been used for social research, applied to investigate people's futures imaginaries or attempting to develop their futures literacy. One approach has built on the popular approach of scenario building that is commonly used in mainstream forecasting practice (Chapter 1). Scenarios involve the construction of narratives (using text or images or both) about possible futures. They are developed to suggest how novel or proposed technologies or services might be used in various

DOI: 10.4324/9781003726579-5

contexts in the future. Speculative fiction scenarios or 'science fiction prototyping' have been used in social futures scholarship to identify possibilities for digitised automation and other emerging digital technologies. Examples are scenarios developed by Birtchnell and Urry (2013) about the futures of 3D printing and McCullagh's (2013) fictional prototype on the possibilities for digital surveillance of chronic disease management. These scenarios were written by the researchers as ways of thinking through alternative futures of these technologies. Other researchers have adopted a more participatory approach, inviting publics to create their own speculative fiction narratives. Jordan and colleagues (2021) engaged engineering teams in speculative fiction workshops to aid their development of solar power technologies and expand their visions to include the sociotechnical aspects of their anticipated innovations. Kaviani and colleagues (2023) developed scenarios from an analysis of industry documents predicting the futures of energy transition, then incorporated insights from their ethnographic fieldwork and workshops with community groups.

Creative writing prompts can be a way to stimulate futures thinking among research participants. A comparative project (Sools et al., 2023) employed the creative writing exercise known as 'Letters from the Future' with 277 residents of 33 countries, most of whom lived in Europe or South and Middle America. The aim was to elicit a personal narrative in which a possible desirable future is imagined as if it had been achieved. Writers were asked to imagine that they had travelled to the future and to write a letter back to the present day. One analysis using this corpus explored the letters crafted by young people from Ecuador and Greece (Gross et al., 2023). The findings showed ambivalent hope on the part of the letter writers about their post-COVID futures, with good outcomes presented as entangled with experiences of loss and struggle. The importance of reassessing values and priorities was emphasised, as was the expression of a desire for social change for better futures rather than a simple return to pre-pandemic lifestyles.

Bringing creative writing prompts together with group discussions is another way to engage research participants in futures thinking. With Ash Watson, I conducted online workshops using this method as part of a research project on people's use and understandings of personal digital data (Lupton & Watson, 2022). The writing prompts we gave participants were designed to invite them to speculate about the futures of data and the devices that generate these data. We wanted to go beyond eliciting matter-of-fact recountings, or responses to direct questions, surfacing the sensory and affective dimensions of their experiences by asking people to think imaginatively. For example, we asked people to imagine what would happen to their personal data when they die, which data they would like to preserve for future generations, and which they would want to delete from archives. They were then asked to share their writing with the rest of the group, sparking discussions. This approach explores not only what participants know about the functions of specific data-generating and automated technologies but also how they might sense, feel and live with these digital media and devices into the future.

Speculative narratives have been used for futures literacy, based on the idea that encouraging people to create narratives about the 'present future' (ideas about futures that shape the present) can inspire them to rethink thought patterns, practice and behaviour in relation to the future. In a project focusing on futures literacy through narrative, Lively and colleagues (2021) used the method of collaborative, character-led performative storytelling to investigate whether people can imagine the future differently if they are doing so through the perspective of an imaginary protagonist rather than as themselves. Participants first developed their characters in isolation and then in conversation with their group, followed by spending time collaboratively devising an imagined world that brought their characters together in a possible future.

Alternate histories and histories of the future are further approaches to creative writing that introduce concepts and method from historical research. In the method of alternate histories (also sometimes referred to as counterfactual histories), a subgenre of science fiction, writers engage with historical events by imagining a different trajectory and outcomes if circumstances are changed. Writers of alternate histories draw on recorded historical facts to focus on constructing a narrative based on the question 'what if' some event in the past did not occur, and how some conditions in the present day would have consequently been altered. The science fiction author Philip K Dick's novel *The Man in the High Castle* is one of the most well-known examples. Set in 1962, the novel presents a dystopian narrative in which the Axis powers (Germany, Italy, Japan) won World War II, imagining what life would be like for people living in a partitioned USA under the rule of Imperial Japan and Nazi Germany (Hellekson, 2001). Historians, philosophers and social scientists have also used counterfactual narratives as thought experiments to help understand the consequences of the chain of events in historical case studies and consider how alternative actions or events may have changed the course of history (Gilbert & Lambert, 2010).

Such thought experiments can be used in futures thinking, as they have implications for identifying what actions or events need to happen in the present or near future to achieve better outcomes. For example, a counterfactual analysis of what would have happened if private ownership of (then new) motor vehicles had been severely restricted in Britain at the start of the twentieth century detailed how citizens would have travelled, what urban infrastructures and services would have been like, how the environment would have been affected and the implications for different social groups of using alternative forms of transport. It was concluded that changes made in the present day to car ownership in Britain may not necessarily lead to fundamental changes in people's everyday mobilities (Pooley, 2010).

Histories of the future involve creating narratives that mimic an historical account, but which focus on events occurring at a future date, written from a perspective of an historian from the future. James Lawrence Powell's book *The 2084 Report: A History of Global Warming from the Future* (2020) is an example of this genre of writing. The book presents interviews with fictional experts from industry, medicine, public health and science, as well as political leaders and ordinary people. Each of these characters reveal the challenges they are facing in the face of environmental degradation, mass extinction, loss of biodiversity and global warming – or what is referred to as 'The Great Warming' in the book – in the year 2084. The author, an academic expert in the field of geochemistry, builds on contemporary scientific research and environmental policy to construct these narratives as a way of warning readers about what will happen to the planet if meaningful action about the climate crisis does not take place in the present. The narratives are not completely nihilistic: some of them also explain what actions may be effective in halting the climate crisis if they are implemented before it is too late.

In another example of histories of the future, Adrian Hon's *A New History of the Future in 100 Objects* (2020) is presented as a museum catalogue of an exhibition in the year 2082. Written from the perspective of the exhibition's curator, a description of each of the 100 objects is presented in chronological order from 2020 to 2082, explaining their purpose, significance and role in the history of the twenty-first century. Some entries are the style of the standard museum catalogue interpretation text, while others have been written as if they are republished blog posts, book excerpts, memoirs, private diaries, news reports, magazine articles or obituaries. The objects include things that were already existing in the year the book was published: for example, the first entry is ankle surveillance monitors for offenders on probation. It then moves on to describe a range of objects that the author has speculated will exist in the decades to come, ranging from new forms of marriage contracts instituted by the European Union in 2046 to cloned meat replacing the practice of killing animals by 2033.

AFROFUTURISM AND INDIGENOUS FUTURISMS

As explained in Chapters 1 and 3, First Nations and non-Western philosophies challenge hegemonic Western concepts of time, highlighting the relational, dynamic, interwoven and non-linear dimensions of more-than-human worlds. The creative and performing arts are often major inspirations for practitioners and scholars of Afrofuturism and Indigenous Futurisms who seek to renew, recover and extend their communities' voices and agencies and their relational connections to the natural world. Science fiction is a key genre in which Afrofuturism and Indigenous Futurisms have been expressed across a range of cultural forms, including literary and popular fiction, video games, cinema and the visual arts.

For many contemporary practitioners and scholars working in the field of decolonisation, Afrofuturism as a speculative creative practice is viewed as a mechanism of survival and a way to find safe spaces for Black people to express both their anger at the oppression they have experienced and their optimism about finding positive ways towards liberation. It offers an alternative viewpoint of Africa and the African diaspora to that presented in colonialist and other Western science fiction, which portrays these places or peoples as only ever located in dystopian futures. It is therefore a way for colonised and racialised Black people to use their knowledge of the past to imagine an inclusive space where transformation can take place (Eseonu & Okoye, 2024; Toliver & Files, 2026).

The work of the influential Black American speculative fiction author Octavia Butler has received renewed attention in recent years, particularly as some of the predictions she outlined in her writing have come to pass. This is perhaps not surprising, given that Butler, one of the first Afrofuturist writers and heralded as a leader in Black feminist science fiction authors, was also a close observer of social trends as well as drawing on history and natural science sources to develop her writing. She was analytical in her speculative fiction, relying on her close observations of contemporary and past events to imagine future worlds. This involved archiving materials and generating connections between them, developing counter-histories and alternative futures that were driven by Butler's radical politics (Streeby, 2018; Toliver & Files, 2026). Butler coined the term 'histofuturism' to describe her method, merging the approach of historians and futurists. She developed an approach that highlighted the research principles of (i) extrapolation ('if this goes on'); (ii) speculation ('what if?'); and (iii) projection ('Take an incident from history and project it into the future') (Streeby, 2018, p. 725).

The Black Quantum Futurism interdisciplinary collective founded by Black Americans Camae Ayewa and Rasheedah Phillips synthesises quantum physics with queer and Afrodiasporic principles to create counter-histories and alternative futures to uplift Black experiences and possibilities (Black Quantum Futurism, 2026). The collective has been involved in community-based projects, performances, workshops, installations, zine making and short films. Phillips' book *Dismantling the Master's Clock: On Race, Space and Time* (2025) brings philosophy, archival research and quantum physics together with her own art and creative writing practice and her activism work on housing policy. As she explains in the book, the non-linear queering of time that is the hallmark of quantum physics can be taken up by Afrofuturist scholars and practitioners to challenge the hegemonic White time conventions that have been imposed on Black people, positioning them as inferior because they do not adhere to clock-time. This is what she means by the title of her book: 'dismantling the master's clock'. Phillips sees quantum time as a way to recuperate non-Western and non-White notions of time and to inspire more equitable frameworks for organising lives and making better futures. Her concept of 'quantum potentiality' offers a way of reclaiming agency over the forces that shape Black and other racialised people's lives and destinies.

For American First Nations (Anishinaabe) cultural critic Grace Dillon, Indigenous science fiction as a form of speculative storytelling operates to affirm Indigenous sovereignty (Dillon & Marques, 2021). She uses the term 'Native slipstream' to encapsulate the ways of thinking about and portraying temporalities in Indigenous Futurisms that bring together space and time as currents flowing together. The concept of the slipstream had first been proposed in the 1970s to describe the experimental writing in which Native American writers were engaged. Dillon also employs the Anishinaabe term *Biskaabiiyang* (returning to the woods) to describe the recovery of ancestral knowledge of the natural world as part of working towards better futures. Dillon discusses another Anishinaabe word, *kobade*, and its meaning of a spiral of intergenerational connections, including the co-presence of spirit persons from the past and the future. She notes that *kobade* differs from the Western science fiction concept of extrapolative future temporalities which mimic a mathematical equation in connecting one dot to another in a linear fashion.

An analysis of Indigenous Okinawan futurism narratives by Kenrick H. Kamiya-Yoshida (2023) identified how Okinawans sought to challenge hegemonic Japanese views of nature and their own culture. Okinawa was once an independent island kingdom until it was invaded by the Japanese settler-colonial state in the early seventeenth century, with the Indigenous residents forced to assimilate into the Japanese value system. When Japanese television and films using science fiction tropes and special effects began to gain prominence in the mid twentieth century, people from islands such as Okinawa were frequently portrayed as uncivilised and subhuman, while other living creatures often featured as destructive villains requiring violent suppression (for example, the well-known figure of Godzilla). To counter these representations, Okinawan television and filmmakers have drawn on their Indigenous cultural values and history to present their own science fiction stories in which their animistic worldview of a more-than-human world where spirits and gods reside everywhere features strongly.

Indigenous Australian researcher Bronwyn Carlson (2026) sees Indigenous Futurisms as offering a pathway of critical hope. In her speculative narrative, she intertwines current global political conditions such as the move towards right and environmental catastrophes with Indigenous cosmologies to converge past and future. Carlson presents a story in which a superstar has exploded into a supernova, emitting cosmic rays that trigger the calling back of Indigenous ancestors to the present to enact retribution against people who have exerted violence or extraction on Country and to restore balance and kinship relations. These guardian figures are empowered by celestial alchemy, reanimating practices and cosmic worldviews that position humans and the more-than-human world as interconnected with time and space. This approach honours the resilience of the ancestors as they fought back against colonial dispossession and exploitation, by creating a more positive future as a collective act of resistance.

SENSORY, AFFECTIVE AND MORE-THAN-HUMAN FUTURING

Taking up arts-based, affective and sensory methods and applying them with more-than-human theoretical perspectives is beginning to gain traction in futures research. This approach can surface the vibrant sensory and affective dimensions of futures and recognise the plasticity and relationality of futures (and of pasts and presents). From this perspective, futures imaginaries are not simply talked or thought about, but are felt in and lived through the body. These futuring techniques can work to make futures seem more tangible when people are imagining what lies ahead. For example, Rebecca Coleman (2017) has outlined a 'sensory sociology of the future' that uses participatory art projects to elicit and uncover the affective and atmospheric aspects of futures.

Tsing's concept of 'arts of noticing' (Chapter 3) has inspired inquiries into the sensory and embodied dimensions of time. As cultural geographer Catherine Phillips (2023) notes, human engagements with other living things can sensitise us to more-than-human temporalities and timescales, including those that extend into the future. She uses the example of her experiences of beekeeping, which involve making time with and for the bees that are cared for in hives. The honeybees have their own rhythms that humans must learn and acknowledge if the colony is to thrive and pests such as the Varroa mite that threatens the continued existence of honeybees is to be managed. Phillips discusses how using her embodied senses helps her to ascertain the health of the hive and quality of the honey the bees are making. Through these close sensory engagements with the bees and the ecosystems in which the human and bees are dwelling, the keeper's body become attuned to the rhythms of the hive. In broader terms, the keeper's observations of the hive and the honey can help attune them to the wider ecological contexts in which the bees are living: including disease, extreme weather events, climate change, associated loss of biodiversity and the ecosocial disaster that will occur due to loss of pollinators, especially honeybees, that support other life on earth.

Astrida Neimanis and Rachel Loewen Walker (2014) have similarly discussed the use of the sensory capacities of their own bodies to observe patterns in the natural world and in weather conditions for future thinking. For Neimanis and Walker, their bodies, memories and the objects that they wear, touch or live with are living records of their encounters with their environments. They suggest applying the concept of 'weathering' (Hamilton et al., 2025) as a bridge between philosophical concepts of human embodiment, weather and climate – including all the nonhuman elements of ecosystems, atmospheres and the infrastructures that part of human-built environments. The process of weathering is a fundamental dimension of existence for humans and other creatures as they move through their lives in relation to the elements and geological features of the natural world. This pursuit involves paying attention to our embodied and affective responses to the weather, climate and ecosystems, as well as acknowledging our kinship with other creatures. For Neimanis and colleagues, weathering is also a call for action in response to environmental degradation and the climate crisis. As Verlie and Neimanis (2023, p. 118) put it, 'We are the climate change we witness'. 'Better modes of weathering' (Hamilton et al., 2025) involve rebuilding the world as a collective pursuit so that both humans and nonhumans can flourish.

Disabled Black Canadian researcher Syrus Marcus Ware (2021) brings together personal reflections from childhood and with nature with the idea of forest bathing, disability justice, decolonising theory and walking pedagogy in his method of 'foraging the future' with young Black people. Ware's intention is to imagine futures where people of colour can survive the ravages of colonialism, capitalism and White supremacy, holding on to a sense of hope. Drawing on disability/crip theory, Octavia Butler's writings and walking practice as research, these imaginings focus on creating a world in which there is the possibility of a 'desired Blackness, a Blackness that is supported as an essential part of all life on this planet' (Ware, 2021, p. 237). Ware's 'foraging the future' method involved walking in a forest with young people of colour from Toronto, using sensory responses to the forest to engage in drawing practices and storytelling, and considering the events that have occurred across deep timescapes in that part of Canada. Through these practices, the young people created embodied knowledge of the landscape and of the histories of dispossession and colonial violence exerted on Indigenous peoples and people of colour, as well as their resistance to this occupation. Ware suggests that these activities can help to prepare young people's minds and bodies for the changes coming in future worlds in which they will be living.

In Chapter 2, the idea of 'thinking with fossilisation' was raised in relation to historical futures theory that de-centres the human subject by engaging with geomaterialities. Another approach involves 'thinking with fermentation', thereby introducing microbial agency into futures thinking. Advocates employ the fermentation metaphor to describe what they perceive to be the dynamic, fizzy, bubbling, even slightly magical transformations that the praxis of fermentation involves (Fournier, 2020; Hamilton & Neimanis, 2018). Human-microbial relations are integral to these fermenting theories and Haraway's 'compost-ist' approach (Chapter 1) is a theoretical inspiration. The bacteria and fungi that work with organic agents to produce chemical reactions that result in fermented beverages, foodstuffs and compost to enrich garden soils that support living creatures, are kin and companion species (Haraway, 2003). Collaborating with humans, they form mutually supportive and expansive partnerships.

Though engaging with microbes in fermentation, humans can conceptualise their bodies' place in the world differently: for example, as living colonies of microbes that are part of their own microbiomes, and the broader ecologies of microbiomes people inhabit. According to Lauren Fournier (2020), fermentation is both a methodology and a metaphor. Drawing on Haraway as well as Jane Bennett's concept of vibrant matter (Chapter 1), Fournier has worked with visual artists, creative writers and researchers to develop the 'fermenting feminism' approach as a methodological framework that embraces queer politics, futurity and inter-species collaborations, involving both care of the self and care for others. Multisensory engagements and materialisations of human-microbial relations are central to these praxes. Advocates of fermentation approaches frequently refer to the sounds, tastes, textures, smells and sights of the rich multispecies assemblages that are created. Indeed, these sensory engagements are required to gauge the progress and wellbeing of the microbial admixtures produced with and through these practices. Fermentation thereby embodies both survival and decomposition, tradition and futurity as part of the microbial processes that support planetary life.

WEIRD, HAUNTED AND SPOOKY FUTURES

In the design research field, speculative design, which engages with the speculative arts and fiction, is one way that futures can be considered creatively. In their landmark book *Speculative Everything* (Dunne & Raby, 2013), Anthony Dunne and Fiona Raby outline how this approach can work as a radical way of imagining how the world could be otherwise and creating discussion. For Dunne and Raby, such activities are not about predicting or forecasting the future – 'trying to pin the future down' (Dunne & Raby, 2013, p. 2) – but rather about imagining a range of possible futures. They see this approach to futures thinking as offering techniques to better understand the present and discuss the kind of futures people want or wish to reject, opening up spaces for debate and discussion. Speculative design methods are therefore deliberately provocative and fictional, developed to encourage viewers to suspend their disbelief and wonder about how things could be.

One way to engage in counter-futuring, weird futuring (Chapter 1) and speculative design is to return to time-honoured lay futuring practices to see what they can offer contemporary research. Horoscopes, crystal balls and other modes of fortune telling have been employed in design research to consider the possible futures of digital technologies. An example drawing on traditional modes of divination is the 'BIY – Believe It Yourself' speculative design fiction developed by the Shanghai-based artistic group automato.farm. It proposes the idea of computers trained by machine learning processes based on vernacular futuring practices and beliefs to help people make daily life decisions and predictions. Traditional divination logics used in this idea include Chinese geomancy and *feng shui*, an Italian folktale about bad luck and Indian numerology and astrology. These provocations are designed to present a blurry border between the present and the future, presenting a project that is close to the mundane reality of the near future and provoking a 'critical aftertaste' in audiences (automato.farm, 2020).

Zine making is another creative approach to explore counter-futures. The AIxDESIGN collective held a zine-making workshop in Rotterdam, the Netherlands, on the theme of esoteric AI as part of its 'Slow AI' project (AI x DESIGN, 2025). The authors note that the blind acceptance of AI can itself be seen as a form of dogma and magical thinking, but is rarely exposed as such due to the hegemony of the Big Tech corporations and the vested interests that support them. The group took inspiration from magic, folklore, divination, fortune telling and other traditional arcane practices to imagine the futures of AI in modes that side-stepped conventional technological predictions about its power and benefits. The creative contributions to the zine used collage and writing to explore novel ways that AI could be either re-enchanted or disenchanted by challenging mainstream boosterism about its supposed quasi magical properties. The workshop used metaphors, symbols and practices from religion, spiritualism and the occult to disrupt the assumption that AI offers better insights, knowledge and foresight than humans. The zine therefore presented alternative ways of seeing, sensing and knowing AI to challenge mainstream perceptions and predictions about its futures: both utopian and dystopian.

In a project on ‘spooky futures’, design researchers (Byrne et al., 2022) engaged with the ethereal, haunted and otherworldly as a way of thinking about the social impacts of novel digital technologies. An inventory of spooky technologies drawn from work across art, design and human computer interaction research was created by the team. They also gathered first-person experiences and conducted interviews with creators as part of the project, investigating what makes certain technological experiences feel unsettling or disturbing, and the contexts of such feelings. The team considered how technologies have often been considered to ‘possessed’ or uncanny: particularly when they are first introduced, and people have little experience with them or understanding of how they work. Telephones, radios and computers (and now generative AI) have all been thought about in this way as people came to terms with how they could be used in everyday life. As noted by this research team, people often feel watched by their devices, as if they have some intention of eavesdropping on them. There are now suggestions that there may be an ‘afterlife’ created for people who have died, using their images and other personal data. Engaging with these examples, the team sought to investigate how people can express feelings of creepiness, dread, paranoia, enchantment or nostalgia for lost futures when they are thinking about technologies, and what the implications are for design futuring.

Hauntological theory has also been incorporated into creative practice together with ethnographic work to contribute insights into the complexities and multiplicities of temporal orderings of the past and futures. Nayrouz Abu Hatoum (2021) drew on her fieldwork with Palestinian artists and creative writers who have imagined and communicated in their work about Palestinian futures as a counter to dominant narratives. She showed that in the face of colonial violence and suffering inflicted by Israel on Palestinians in their daily life, involving tight control over how they can spend their time (for example, the imposition of checkpoints), the Palestinian struggle for liberation is always already future-oriented. Through the artists' and writers' work, Abu Hatoum demonstrates that Palestinian temporality can be viewed as cyclical rather than linear, in which there are multiple points of beginnings, due to the long-term and replicating violence and dispossession to which they have been subjected. Therefore, in Palestinians' decolonial imaginaries of the future, there is a tension between suspicion and hope, in which 'the future might evoke a past or haunt the present' (Abu Hatoum, 2021, p. 409).

SPECULATIVE PEDAGOGIES

In education research, the term 'speculative pedagogies' is used to describe adopting a speculative stance in teaching, learning and pedagogical research. This approach involves using speculative writing prompts, speculative design or experimental making to envision alternatives to the present conditions, including those that are more socially just or empathetic and can expand capacities for learning and knowledge production. There is an emphasis on generating counter-narratives that challenge normative notions of futures as well as developing a 'critical hope' stance that is neither dystopian nor utopian (Ross, 2026; Tomin & Collis, 2023).

In one example of a speculative pedagogies study, Canadian researchers drew on Haraway's speculative fabulation concept (Chapter 1) to work with Toronto secondary school students from diverse ethnic heritages in a collaborative world-building project related to environmental futures (Tomin & Collis, 2023). They used science fiction narratives and storytelling approaches to develop counter-narratives of future possibilities in their city. The 'Toronto 2049' project was created through a collaborative wiki-style catalogue of the future. Based on the realities of the present, students were asked to envision possible futures together, addressing questions such as what did they think the city would likely look like? What did they want it to look like, and how did they want it to feel to live in that future? What did they fear? Using the stories created through this process, students were engaged in conversations about their hopes and fears for the future that reached beyond neoliberal visions of progress, change, innovation and productivity to develop narratives of critical hope.

In her project, Jen Ross (2026) adopted the method of speculative heritage thinking as a way to inspire postgraduate education students from culturally diverse backgrounds at the University of Edinburgh to imagine the futures of lifelong learning. A fiction-based task was designed as an assignment for the course, in which the students were asked to write a 'story from the future' related to a lifelong learning key issue. They were asked to include at least one heritage object, intangible practice or site into the story, designed to embed their speculative thinking into specific dimensions of meanings and values of past things, places or practices with which they had strong connections. Examples of heritage objects that students incorporated into their stories from the future included: a clothes chest or Filipino *baul* containing hidden recordings from a narrator's ancestors, plants and seeds from a gene bank, and a grand colonial building in Nairobi. This approach to speculative narrative offered a way of promoting futures thinking as a more material and less abstract endeavour, as well as encouraging students to engage with their memories and embodied and sensory experiences.

In a project drawing on Haraway's concept of speculative fabulation and Tsing's concept of the arts of noticing, researchers, teachers and artists worked with English school children to construct sculptures made of discarded plastic objects (Kraftl, 2022). The plastic objects were collected by the artists working with the children from local public spaces where they were discarded, as well as recycling sites and charity shops. The children were asked to create vertical sculptures by placing a selection of these items onto a tall, thin metal spike, responding to prompts such as 'build a sculpture that looks good' or 'build one that orders stuff from "useless" to "useful"'. The intention of this project was to encourage them to contemplate the role of plastic 'waste' objects in their everyday lives, the plastics' potentially positive value and what the environmental impacts of these objects may be into the future. The process also engaged the children in storytelling about these items to provoke reflections about alternative ways of relating to or sensing plastics.

Black American education researcher Jillian Ford used a Black feminist hauntological lens to explore ways to imagine new futures with adults. She co-created the Cosmic Curriculum with fellow community members in a city in southern USA. This was a project designed to engage with the spirits of Black antebellum ancestors who resisted dehumanisation by embodying refusals of liberalism and its material consequences in the form of colonialism and slavery. The Cosmic Curriculum involved a series of community workshops conducted in public parks. Participants created artworks with natural materials and engaged in stargazing, storytelling and other collective practices. They reflected on haunting on the land on which they gathered of colonialism, Indigenous genocide, land dispossession and enslavement, engaging with elements of the park's ecosystem (plants, sticks, stones, soil) to wonder about the past lives of these non-human things. These reflections were then used to mourn lost futures but then generate ideas about what might change if participants honoured their ancestors' spirits and attuned more closely to the natural world to create new possibilities for mutual flourishing.

Shae Brown (2023) has used Indigenous cosmologies of spiral time and pattern and fractal thinking (Chapter 1) in her teaching at Australian secondary schools. She begins by prompting students to consider 'what is time?' and 'If time as a straight line is a recent invention, how else is time conceptualised?'. They are invited to think about their own lives and experiences of time and change, exploring how time seems to stop and start, go backwards or forwards, so that they can begin to conceptualise themselves as 'complex time-beings'. The young people are then introduced to ecological and fractal patterning, metaphors of temporalities based on weather, atmosphere, soil conditions and other species, and entanglement to identify spiral time patterning as part of the complexities and unpredictability of life. Brown includes activities such as considering the oldest seed ever sprouted and grown, and how this example enacts the potential future as already present, in the now-past and manifest in the present-now. For Brown, this approach is a generative approach to encouraging students to think about and express complex temporal concepts beyond hegemonic time, and to apply it to their own lives.

CURATION, ART, MUSEOLOGY AND FUTURES

The practices of museology and curation have traditionally been understood as ways of preserving artefacts from past eras as a form of remembrance and education, offering portals into previous lifetimes or eras of Earth's natural history. However, there is also a long history of museums offering insights into future worlds: either as exhibition spaces within a museum or in museums dedicated solely to future worldbuilding. In recent times, museums have also been portraying themselves as sites for developing futures literacy among visitors; or as Kristin Alford (2024, p. 3) puts it 'building community capabilities' so that members of the public can be 'better at futures thinking'.

Since the mid-nineteenth century, there have been regular temporary world exhibitions or expositions, often described as 'World's Fairs' or 'Expos', devoted to the curation of futuristic ideas, with developments in new technologies and industries regularly featuring as part of speculative worldbuilding. Most of these exhibitions have been overtly driven as promotional, oriented towards supporting economic and industry development through new technologies, with a clear political agenda to highlight certain nations' or cultures' supposed superiority in innovation (Shulruff & Wyman, 2023). Many museums of the future (also often called 'museums of tomorrow') now offer a similar experience. For example, Dubai's Museum of the Future (2025) advertises itself as a 'beacon of hope', a 'home for optimistic imagination, committed to a more sustainable future for all', with 'our imagined futures rooted in the values of the UAE [United Arab Emirates] and the Arab world'. We can readily see echoes here of the discourses used in World's Fairs in the unabashed national promotion in this museum's website, positioning the museum/ UAE as leading the world (indeed 'humanity') in new ideas and technological development with 'values' that are clearly articulated as contextualised to UAE and Arab world.

Such museums tend to promote a social imaginary of futures that are tightly controlled by the museum funders and curators. Visitors are invited to engage with the exhibits in highly constricted ways that leave little room for the development of counter-futuring, reflections on social, postcolonial, ecological and multispecies justice or other forms of creative futuring (Guasco, 2020). A more critical approach positions museums as political storytelling institutions that operate to promote the vested visions of the future of the individuals or organisations who fund them (traditionally governments or wealthy philanthropic donors). As such, the narratives presented in museums' collections are affective and embodied experiences that have political consequences for how visitors imagine futures (Guasco, 2020). Consequently, some scholars have argued for the need to 'queer museums' in ways that counter their dominant conventions and practices. From this position, museums and museological practice are reimagined as sites where curators and visitors can participate in socially transformative ways of seeing, knowing, being and doing: including those that can generate progressive and radical visions of the future (Sullivan & Middleton, 2019).

Challenging the archetypal model of the museum of the future, design researchers have put forward the model of the 'Futures Lab'. Such labs are envisaged as participatory spaces where diverse voices can be included to craft plural futures, as well as incorporating the more-than-human world and multisensory and affective experiments. The importance of localised and contextualised participation in futures thinking is key to this model. In one example, researchers reflected on their experiences at a World Expo in Dubai, drawing attention to the successful use of sensory experience in some of the national pavilions but also highlighting the lack of interactive experiences, connections to the more-than-human world, cross-temporal content that acknowledges the relationship between the past, present and future, or overt recognition of past and continuing social justice issues. These injustices include the hidden labour performed by labourers from countries such as the Philippines who are contributing to the rapid development of Dubai as a city of the future but are subjected to poor working conditions (Shulruff & Wyman, 2023).

Museologists and exhibition curators have also begun to question the chrononormativity of the typical museum display and the temporal assumptions underpinning curation. These approaches are underpinned by the idea that time is not only measured but is also made through social and cultural practice, and that museums are key cultural sites where temporalities are contested and configured. The objects and interpretation displays in museums are lively, bearing affective forces and potentially opening capacities for action and seeing otherwise. Museum things therefore have a future-assembling capacity, operating as 'transtemporal nodes' which function as 'more-than-human materializing storage devices' (Fredengren et al., 2025, p. 123). By curating time differently in new modes of museology, the diversities of temporalities across multi-species relationships, power dynamics and geographical settings can be brought to the fore (Fredengren & Owman, 2024; Fredengren et al., 2025).

An analysis by Christina Fredengren and colleagues (2025) of the role of museums in cultural heritage built on Bennett's scholarship on enchantment and thing-power (Chapter 1). They argue that in developing their collections, practices of conservation and programming, museums should include questions about more-than-human, intragenerational justice and care of the objects in their possession. Fredengren and colleagues provide case studies of artefacts in museums in Sweden, placing them in a more-than-human ecological context. One instance involved investigating a soil sample derived from an excavation of an Iron Age burial site in central Sweden. Through DNA analysis of the soil, the researchers identified how this soil bears witness to and carries the material memory of organic and geological processes, human remains and material culture (burial practices and offerings), as well as radical transformations in the environment since the Iron Age. Paying attention to the relations between these things, the natural histories of their lives and their associations with humans and museum practices offers a rich way to understand how such objects have thing-power in the past, present and emerging futures (see also the discussion of palimpsestic time in Chapter 2).

Museum collections, displays and interpretation materials can be curated in ways that inspire imaginative engagements from visitors to help them engage in futures-thinking. The concept of the 'relational museum' builds on this idea by creating the conditions by which transformation in thinking about the future may occur by bringing objects, stories and people together as a form of material storytelling (Newell et al., 2016). To fully acknowledge the museum's overt role as a storytelling agent (and potential force for social change), wall texts and other materials that highlight their past roles in promoting the opinions and futures visions of powerful people and organisations, while excluding others, must be part of its activities (Guasco, 2020). This was an approach used in the Manchester Museum's exhibition 'Climate Control' in 2015–2016, with activities developed by academics from the University of Manchester with the Manchester Climate Change Agency and a range of non-government and community organisations. The exhibition had two entrances where visitors could choose either to explore climate change in the past (and present) or the future. The connection between events over deep timescales and between far-distant places was emphasised in the 'past/present' section of the exhibition. The 'explore the future' space provided information on climate change action at local, national and international scales, together with activities inviting people to share ideas on 'changing the future' and to reflect on the ideas of others (McGhie et al., 2020).

Artmaking provides compelling views into the future. Artists have acted as 'seers, soothsayers, communicators, and elucidators', using 'radically creative approaches to documenting ruptures in the fabric of the natural world' (Cohen et al., 2023, p. 14). Art installations bring three-dimensional effects and multimedia that can engage audiences' senses in compelling ways to help them imagine possible futures. For instance, Zane Griffin Talley Cooper's 'Alchemical Infrastructures: Making Blockchain in Iceland', addresses how bitcoin and other cryptocurrency are 'mined' in the quest for new monetary futures as a form of contemporary alchemy. This piece, with its focus on the situated nature of the data centre infrastructure in Iceland, demonstrates the limitations of metrics that purport to demonstrate the environmental impacts of cryptocurrency infrastructures by focusing solely on quantifying emissions. It involves bringing together ethnographic research to examine what blockchain looks, feels, sounds and smells like in an experimental documentary film, a soundscape and a photo series. Through these artistic interventions, data centre and cloud computing infrastructures are made visible, tangible and audible.

Counter-futuring and queer futuring can also be facilitated with and through immersive exhibitions using a range of different media, performances, artworks and artefacts. In an example of such an approach, the mixed reality exhibit 'Museum of Austerity' in London 2025–2026 drew on the notion of witnessing by presenting holographic performances by professional actors enacting the testimonies of people with disabilities' experiences of living through austerity. The show is based on the stories recounted by their relatives of eight people who died as a consequence of being denied welfare benefits. A theatre was transformed into a holographic gallery through which audiences moved wearing a mixed reality headset. Participating in this exhibition, audience members were challenged to confront how the UK government's winding back of social support for people living with disability has led to poverty, starvation and illness, and to consider the future impacts of government policy and the failure of safety nets on people's lives (Akbar, 2025).

Some artists and researchers have experimented with using traditional modes of divination and fortune telling as a method of socially engaged art involving social interaction and the collective exchange of ideas. This is art-making not just as an act of representation, but as a mode of social inquiry and collective labour that can contribute to other ways of seeing the future of current crises. The traditional practice of esoteric tarot is one such lay futuring practice that has received attention from artists, activists and scholars. Australian artist and researcher Anastasia Murney (2023) has reflected on the use of tarot in creative practice addressing the climate crisis. She notes that tarot can be used to evoke affective and heuristic responses, operating in pedagogical but also therapeutic ways. Each tarot card can be used in combination as a provocation; the symbolic and allegorical language of the traditional cards being used to find ways to use in a group setting to invite affective responses that can recast a problem in novel formulations and uncover new connections and patterns.

In other arts-based reinventions of tarot, the arts futurist organisation founded and run by artists based in Nairobi, Kairos Futura, offers an online 'Wild Story Generator' speculative game (Kairos Futura, 2025). Based on tarot-inspired prompts designed by the collective, the game helps people imagine new futures that are located in their own dwelling place and related to the community-level challenges they face. Artist and academic, American Alexandro Segade (2025), has designed a tarot card deck together with his artistic collective, My Barbarian, which includes performances inspired by interpretations of the cards. The first suit of the deck features images of cats to draw attention to the tradition of feline mysticism but also the close relationship between humans and cats as both living creatures and part of the more-than-human world. One card, for example, features a three-headed cat goddess, referencing creativity and destruction with meanings of profound transformation, while another features cats as action heroes and activists, symbolising triumph, domination and colonisation.

Art exhibition curation also offers opportunities to portray creative futuring ideas and cosmologies that challenge hegemonic temporalities by programming the work of artists who have traditionally been excluded or marginalised in major galleries, including Indigenous artists and those from the Global South. One example is the work exhibited in 'Everywhen: The Eternal Present in Indigenous Art from Australia' at Harvard Museums, USA, in 2016 (Gilchrist, 2016). The exhibition was curated to provoke visitors to think about temporalities through an Indigenous lens and thus imagine the world otherwise, beyond clock time. The everywhen paradigm (Chapter 1) was used in the exhibition through four themes: seasonality, transformation, performance and remembrance. One of the works featured in the Seasonality gallery was Emily Kam Kngwarray's four-panelled work *'Anwerlarr Angerr'* (big yam). These paintings depict the subtle transitions between seasons associated with the growth and ripening of the pencil yam in the artist's Country (the Central Desert). They bring together manifestations of ancestral presence and women's ceremonial and food-gathering responsibilities with concepts of fertility and continued abundance and kinship with Country.

The 'After the Rain' 5th Indigenous Art Triennial shown at the National Museum of Australia (2025) featured stories of both despair and hope related to the experiences of Australian First Nations peoples related to their cultural stories and relations with Country and the violence wrought by exploitation since the European settlers arrived on the continent. The metaphor of 'after the rain' was used by artistic director Tony Albert to represent the cyclical renewal of more-than-human worlds following life-giving rain after prolonged periods of dry weather in desert regions. This metaphor was particularly encapsulated in the final exhibit in the show, featuring fabric sculptures by Yarrenyty Arltere Artists' fabric sculptures. These sculptures rejoice in the elemental power of rain, as a transformative and cleansing renewal force for Culture and Country. The central sculpture, 'Beautiful *Ulkumanu* (old woman), After the Rain', is a tall female figure embroidered with wildflowers and carrying edible plants, representing the bounty of Country after rainfall. As visitors leave the exhibition, they are greeted with an archway of other textile sculptures through which they are invited to depart by *Ulkumanu*, with a farewell blessing and invitation to 'just feel what you are feeling from this beautiful exhibition and let that be memory to stay with you when step out and off you go'.

Exhibitions such as these can introduce visitors to the chronodiversity of cultures other than their own and the integral bonds of relationality that underpin non-Western worldviews of how past, present and future are intertwined. They offer a 'deep horizons' perspective, pushing the limits of human vision and thought beyond the past and present towards imagining more ethically durable, emotionally invested and inhabitable futures (Cohen et al., 2023).

REFERENCES

Abu Hatoum, N. (2021). Decolonizing [in the] future: Scenes of Palestinian temporality. *Geografiska Annaler: Series B, Human Geography*, *103*(4), 397–412.

AI x DESIGN. (2025). Esoteric AI. https://aixdesign.co/posts/esoteric-ai

Akbar, A. (2025, December 11). Museum of Austerity review - a devastating reckoning with Britain's decade of neglect. *The Guardian*. https://www.theguardian.com/stage/2025/dec/11/museum-of-austerity-review-a-devastating-reckoning-with-britains-decade-of-neglect

Alford, K. (2024). Building community capabilities in futures thinking. In K. Alford (Ed.), *Cultivating futures thinking in museums* (pp. 3–9). Routledge.

automato.farm. (2020). BIY - Believe It Yourself. *Spooky Technology.* https://spookyte.ch/inventory/biy-believe-it-yourself/

Birtchnell, T., & Urry, J. (2013). 3D, SF and the future. *Futures, 50*, 25–34.

Black Quantum Futurism. (2026). *Black Quantum Futurism.* https://www.blackquantumfuturism.com/about

Brown, S. L. (2023). Teaching complex time through pattern thinking and understanding. *Time & Society, 32*(3), 336–358.

Byrne, D., Lockton, D., Hu, M., Luong, M., Ranade, A., Escarcha, K., Giesa, K., Huang, Y., Yochum, C., Robertson, G., Yeung, L., Cruz, M., Danner, C., Wang, E., Khurana, M., Chen, Z., Heyison, A., & Fu, Y. (2022). *Spooky Technology: The ethereal and otherworldly as a resource for design. Designing Interactive Systems Conference*, Virtual Event, Australia.

Carlson, B. (2026). Ancestors on motorbikes: Cosmic rays bring retribution. *Continuum*, https://doi.org/10.1080/10304312.2025.2544785

Cohen, B., Espelie, E., & Etherington, B. (2023). Introduction. In B. Cohen, E. Espelie, & B. Etherington (Eds.), *Deep horizons: A multisensory archive of ecological affects and prospects.* Amherst College Press.

Coleman, R. (2017). A sensory sociology of the future: Affect, hope and inventive methodologies. *The Sociological Review, 65*(3), 525–543.

Dillon, G. L., & Marques, P. N. (2021). Taking the fiction out of science fiction: A conversation about indigenous futurisms. *e-flux Journal, 120.* https://www.e-flux.com/journal/120/417043/taking-the-fiction-out-of-science-fiction-a-conversation-about-indigenous-futurisms

Dunne, A., & Raby, F. (2013). *Speculative everything: Design, fiction, and social dreaming.* The MIT Press.

Eseonu, T., & Okoye, F. (2024). Making a case for Afrofuturism as a critical qualitative inquiry method for liberation. *Public Integrity, 26*(6), 674–685.

Fournier, L. (2020). Fermenting feminism as methodology and metaphor: Approaching transnational feminist practices through microbial transformation. *Environmental Humanities, 12*(1), 88–112.

Fredengren, C., Ewing, A., Owman, C., & Holmstedt, J. (2025). Museum ecologies: Museum things as guides for how to deal with ecological challenges in the Anthropocene. *Museum & Society*, 23(1). https://journals.le.ac.uk/index.php/mas/article/view/4698

Fredengren, C., & Owman, C. (2024). Curating time – Museum-things as counterclocks in a climate-challenged world. *Time & Society*, 33(1), 95–117.

Gilbert, D., & Lambert, D. (2010). Counterfactual geographies: Worlds that might have been. *Journal of Historical Geography*, 36(3), 245–252.

Gilchrist, S. (2016). *Everywhen: The eternal present in Indigenous art from Australia*. Yale University Press. https://yalebooks.yale.edu/2016/09/21/everywhen-the-eternal-present-in-indigenous-art-from-australia/

Gross, J., Davids, T., Sools, A., & Saghai, Y. (2023). COVID-19 and the politics of hope: A comparative analysis of Greek and Ecuadorian letters from a desired post-pandemic future. *Futures*, 149. https://doi.org/10.1016/j.futures.2023.103115

Guasco, A. (2020). As dead as a dodo': Extinction narratives and multispecies justice in the museum. *Environment and Planning E: Nature and Space*, 4(3), 1055–1076.

Hamilton, J. M., & Neimanis, A. (2018). Composting feminisms and environmental humanities. *Environmental Humanities*, 10(2), 501–527.

Hamilton, J. M., Neimanis, A., & Campo, E. (2025). An infrastructural politics for climate change adaptation, via weather: Interview by Enrico Campo with Jennifer Mae Hamilton and Astrida Neimanis. *Journal of Classical Sociology*, 25(2), 206–221.

Haraway, D. (2003). *The companion species manifesto: Dogs, people, and significant otherness*. Prickly Paradigm.

Hellekson, K. (2001). *The alternate history: Refiguring historical time*. Kent State University Press.

Hon, A. (2020). *A new history of the future in 100 objects: A fiction*. MIT Press.

Jordan, M., Bernier, J., & Zuiker, S. (2021). The future is open and shapable: Using solar speculative fiction to foster learner agency. *Literacy Research: Theory, Method, and Practice*, 70(1), 309–329.

Kairos Futura. (2025). *Wild Story Generator*. https://wildfuturegenerator.thefutureisonearth.org/story

Kamiya-Yoshida, K. H. (2023). "Okinawa Q" (an Uchinanchū futurism): Okinawans rectify the Japanese unbalanced view of nature through Tokusatsu television and film. In T.T. Taylor, I. Lavender III, G.L. Dillon, & B. Chattopadhyay (Eds.), *The Routledge handbook of coFuturisms* (pp. 176–185). Routledge.

Kaviani, F., Strengers, Y., Dahlgren, K., Korsmeyer, H., & Pink, S. (2023). Building plausible scenarios for future living: Intervening in energy forecasting using household ethnography and foresight. *Energy Research & Social Science, 106*. https://doi.org/10.1016/j.erss.2023.103315

Kraftl, P. (2022). Speculating with childhoods, plastics and other stuff. In N. Williams & T. Keating (Eds.), *Speculative geographies: Ethics, technologies, aesthetics* (pp. 187–202). Springer Nature Singapore.

Liveley, G., Slocombe, W., & Spiers, E. (2021). Futures literacy through narrative. *Futures, 125*. https://www.sciencedirect.com/science/article/pii/S0016328720301531

Lupton, D., & Watson, A. (2022). Research-creations for speculating about digitized automation: Bringing creative writing prompts and vital materialism into the sociology of futures. *Qualitative Inquiry*, *28*(7), 754–766.

McCullagh, P. (2013). Superhighway patrolman. *Futures, 50*, 101–108.

McGhie, H., Mander, S., & Minns, A. (2020). The time machine: Challenging perceptions of time and place to enhance climate change engagement through museums. *Museum & Society, 18*(2), 183–217.

Murney, A. (2023). Tarot as affective cartography in the uneven anthropocene. *Journal of Visual Culture*, 22(2), 243–263.

Museum of the Future. (2025). About us. https://museumofthefuture.ae/en/about-us

National Museum of Australia. (2025). *5th National Indigenous Art Triennial: After the Rain*. https://nga.gov.au/exhibitions/fifth-national-indigenous-art-triennial/

Neimanis, A., & Walker, R. L. (2014). Weathering: Climate change and the "thick time" of transcorporeality. *Hypatia*, *29*(3), 558–575.

Newell, J., Robin, L., & Wehner, K. (2016). Introduction: Curating connections in a climate-changed world. In J. Newell, L. Robin, & K. Wehner (Eds.), *Curating the future: Museums, communities and climate change* (pp. 25–40). Routledge.

Phillips, C. (2023). Making time for and with honeybees. In A. Franklin (Ed.), *The Routledge international handbook of more-than-human studies* (pp. 322–333). Routledge.

Phillips, R. (2025). *Dismantling the Master's clock: On race, space, and time*. AK Press.

Pooley, C. G. (2010). Landscapes without the car: A counterfactual historical geography of twentieth-century Britain. *Journal of Historical Geography*, *36*(3), 266–275.

Powell, J. L. (2020). *The 2084 report: A novel of the great warming*. Simon and Schuster.

Ross, J. (2026). Stories from the future of lifelong learning: Fiction, technology and speculative pedagogies. *Learning, Media and Technology*. https://doi.org/10.1080/17439884.2025.2591697

Segade, A. (2025). Cat suit (minor arcana). *ASAP Review*. https://asapjournal.com/node/cat-suit-minor-arcana/

Shulruff, T., & Wyman, L. (2023). A trip through Tomorrowland: The world expo as futures lab. *World Futures Review*, *15*(1), 22–37.

Sools, A., Saghai, Y., & Gross, J. (2023). 'Will the world never be the same?' Everyday imaginaries of post-corona futures. *Futures*, *153*. https://www.sciencedirect.com/science/article/pii/S0016328723001386

Streeby, S. (2018). Radical reproduction: Octavia E. Butler's histofuturist archiving as speculative theory. *Women's Studies*, *47*(7), 719–732.

Sullivan, N., & Middleton, C. (2019). *Queering the Museum*. Routledge.

Toliver, S. R., & Files, M. (2026). Kindred rites of Sankofa: On Octavia Butler's histofuturist approach to artful inquiry. *Qualitative Inquiry*, *32*(2), 182–189.

Tomin, B., & Collis, R. B. (2023). Science fiction, speculative pedagogy, and critical hope: Counternarratives for/of the future. In *Reimagining science education in the Anthropocene, Volume 2* (pp. 247–265). Springer International Publishing Cham.

Verlie, B., & Neimanis, A. (2023). Breathing climate crises. *Angelaki*, *28*(4), 117–131.

Ware, S. M. (2021). Foraging the future: Forest baths, engaged pedagogy, and planting ourselves into the future. *Qualitative Inquiry*, *28*(2), 236–243.

CONCLUSION

Throughout this book, the nature and meaning of professional and mundane futuring practices across historical eras and cultures have been shown to be complex and dynamic. Futuring practices have been positioned as assemblages of systems and networks of actors, beliefs, acculturated habits, actions and discourses that are passed on through generations. They are specific to time and place but are also fluid, contingent and subject to change and reinvention. Diverse conceptualisations and experiences of temporalities – linear, clock, queer, deep, circular, spiral, patterned, quantum, fractal, palimpsestic, thick, haunted – have received attention. I have explored the role played by hegemonic time, together with social and economic forces such as capitalism, globalisation, colonialism and neoliberalism, in structuring and shaping lay futuring beliefs and practices for individuals and social groups. I have demonstrated that futures thinking has many purposes: it can be a profession, a form of social control, a way to achieve better self-understanding or a radical practice aimed at showing care about others or the natural world.

The historical and contemporary research covered in the book has demonstrated that across cultures, expert and lay futuring practices are part of complex belief systems incorporating religion, magic, the occult, mysticism and the supernatural, based on the premise that

DOI: 10.4324/9781003726579-6

external forces propel human destinies. It has illustrated that human societies have long combined expert knowledge and customs with lay or folk beliefs and practices in attempting to access the future, and that there has been a regular exchange of these beliefs and practices between cultures. The book has further demonstrated that bringing together creatures and objects, place and space with futuring beliefs generates powerful affective forces and atmospheres that motivate human behaviour and decision-making. Mention has been made of astrology, augury, omen, dream and prodigy interpretation, extispicy, haruspicy, geomancy, necromancy, scrying, tarot reading and other forms of cartomancy, palmistry, physiognomy, sieve driving, coffee cup reading, dice casting, the use of charms, incantations, prayers to the gods and amulets, *feng shui*, spiritualism, seances and almanacs. Such practices include a variety of objects taken from nature and those that have been made or modified by humans. Whether it is rocks, plants, animal intestines and bones, glaciers, birds, hallucinogenic substances, celestial bodies, crystal balls, dice, charms, spells, cards, printed manuscripts or digital technologies such as websites, chatbots and apps, these things are part of magical performances and rites incorporated into people's lives.

These futuring assemblages of objects, place, people, customs, rituals and creatures have symbolic and social structural value, contributing to the leadership and governance of societies, the maintenance of social cohesion and the passing on of culture. Futuring assemblages are also central to meaning making in people's everyday lives. They are not necessarily nor solely about prediction of people's destinies. Far more than this, futuring is a way of knowing and being, for meeting the desire for certainty in uncertain times, managing risk, assisting with decision-making, peering into the unknown, allowing people to express their anxieties and fears and helping them clarify their thoughts and feelings about the fickleness of life. Everyday futuring practices are often pragmatic ways that people make sense of the world in which they live, ascribe moral meanings to their past experiences and to futures or contemplate their relationships with other humans and with other-than-human beings in ways that go beyond quotidian experience. It is for these reasons that even in historical periods when authorities have tried to repress or banish lay futuring practices, they have quickly returned – often becoming more popular than ever.

Building on the insights on chronodiversity and temporal experiences offered in this book, researchers can investigate how people in specific socioeconomic and geographical contexts think about futures in relation to their general beliefs about time. Practices that are current today have a history but also potentially a momentum that reaches into the future. We can ponder how our lived experiences of the past and the present have shaped how we imagine futures and envision counter-futures. Working with Afrofuturism, Indigenous, queer, feminist, radical, spooky and weird futurisms, we can think about how resistance can be mounted to the attempts of the powerful to shape others' futures, including engaging in speculative fabulations that help us to think otherwise. We can think about how concrete utopias may be generated through struggle, helping hope and wonder to re-emerge from sites of despair.

These initiatives involve acknowledging the encoding and embeddedness of knowledge into human bodies, tangible things and intangible phenomena such as ancestral spirits, and the responsibilities of humans to all the creatures and other entities (land, sky, water) that constitute landscapes. We can begin to identify the materialities of 'making time' – including how futures are made. These approaches provoke questions such as: How to disrupt and think beyond (or queer) mainstream Western notions of the linearity of time? Where do the past, present and future begin and end? Where are these boundaries blurred? How do we live and walk alongside the past and the future? How do intra-actions with things, place and space generate temporalities? How do people seek to trick time? What timespaces do they share with others (human and nonhuman)? Where is time thickened or thinned?

To answer these questions, researchers could ask people to take photos of objects or images that represent the ways they conceptualise and experience time, create a collage that involves layering things and places to represent palimpsestic or deep time, or invite people to respond to a creative writing prompt that invites them to craft an alternate history, counterfactual or a narrative about the history of the future. We might use prompts with research participants such as: 'If you could design the next Seven Wonders of the World – what would they be?'. 'Design a fossil of the future'. 'Imagine you are an archaeologist 200 years into the future. What kinds of artefacts would you be uncovering and trying to piece together to get a sense of human life in this day and age?'. 'Create a catalogue of commonly used digital devices from the year 2050'. 'Write a travel article about a trip you will take 30 years from now'. 'Create a recipe book for dishes people will be consuming in the year 2130'.

Developing our arts of noticing, we can engage in more-than-human and sensory futures thinking by attuning ourselves to the elements and acknowledging our kinship with the other species and landscapes in which we dwell. We can ask the questions: How do sensory and embodied experiences of sociomaterialities contribute to how people imagine futures? What will the smells, tastes, sights, feelings and sounds of the future be? How do we imagine futures as part of multispecies worlds located in diverse physical environments and geographical regions? How do we demonstrate kinship and care with all living things and the natural world in our approach to future thinking? What assemblages of objects, creatures, practices and humans generate enchantment and thing-power that help us look forward and motivate us to act on these visions? What are the sites where these intra-actions are particularly potent, opening up capacities for action and for human and more-than-human flourishing?

To prod creative thinking towards these directions, we can engage in weathering, thinking with fossils, geology and deep timescapes, or with microbes, composting and fermentation. We can encourage people to use their senses to notice patterns of change in their environments and how these changes make them feel in their bodies – air and water quality, weather, rainfall, seasonal turns, building and infrastructure (for example, the presence or quality of footpaths, roads and buildings). We can help them consider how these embodied, multisensory observations attune us to temporalities and how we share these temporalities with companion species. We can encourage them to notice fermenting or decomposing matter, erosion and synergistic relationships to consider the dynamic spiral and cyclical dimensions of time. Practices of mapping, photography, journaling, drawing and creative writing can help people document their observations and make connections between what they see and feel when inhabiting these more-than-human worlds.

Engaging with historical perspectives is a way of bringing together disparate forms of knowledges and temporalities. We can also return to the past to consider how traditional customs might provide inspirations for researching futures thinking and developing new methods that build on old ways. How might we revive the magical imagination? How, as researchers, can we think with augury, scrying, necromancy, geomancy or astrology? What are the contemporary omens and portents from the natural world we might use to divine our futures? We could ask participants to make a zine or write a poem or short story about using dice, a crystal ball, *feng shui* or astrology to predict an everyday event in their life. We could encourage them to design a grimoire (book of magic) including their own spells, invent amulets or incantations for predicting the future, make an almanac for a future year, craft a version of Zodiac Man for the contemporary era or invent a new set of tarot cards that build on their ideas of what symbols are most meaningful to help them imagine their futures.

Pondering the power of affective forces and thinking with the notion of palimpsestic time and hauntology, participants and researchers can identify the affective atmospheres and layers of the places in which we dwell and through which we move as we go through our lives. We can think about how these atmospheres contribute to the ways we feel and imagine futures. We can acknowledge that our ancestors' knowledge, customs and experiences live with us and extend into the present. We also need to recognise that our relationships with other kin – with the creatures, water, air and land with which we share this planet – are incorporated into hauntologies and affective atmospheres. For our research, we can consider: What places, spaces and things generate atmospheres of futures? What haunts us into and about the future? What are the ghosts of futures past? How do feelings of spookiness, the uncanny or weirdness provoke us to think otherwise about futures? Where are other living beings in these hauntings and atmospheres?

With and through these provocations and creative futuring methods, we can activate affective, embodied and multisensory ways of living futures. We can begin to imagine the cracks and crannies through which humans and our companion species can grow, extend ourselves towards the light and flourish.

INDEX

For Product Safety Concerns and Information please contact our EU representative GPSR@taylorandfrancis.com
Taylor & Francis Verlag GmbH, Kaufingerstraße 24, 80331 München, Germany

www.ingramcontent.com/pod-product-compliance
Lightning Source LLC
Chambersburg PA
CBHW070726280726
48882CB00027B/595
* 9 7 8 1 0 4 1 2 1 3 0 8 6 *